AF411155

PETER ZIMMERMANN

GALERIE PERROTIN 貝浩登

New York - Paris - Hong Kong

紐約 - 巴黎 - 香港

DAMIANI

Interview with Marietta Franke
與瑪瑞埃塔 ‧ 弗蘭卡對談

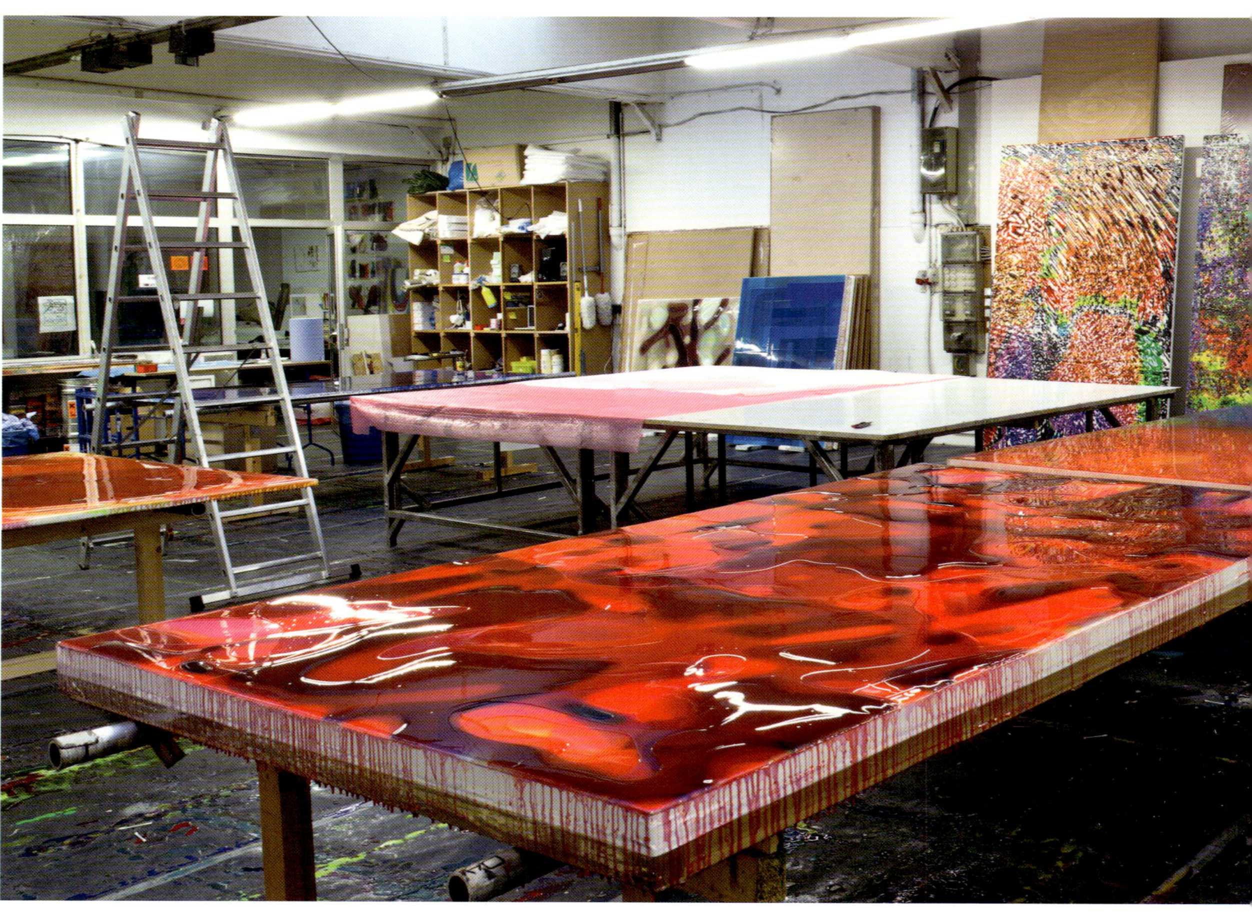

*About paintings that compete for perception, cohesion rather than fragmentation,
and the luxury of the painter*

Marietta Franke   We are meeting in your Cologne studio to talk about the paintings
that have come out of the last four years. "Paintings lead their own life". Would you consider a phrase
such as "Paintings want something" to be valid?

Peter Zimmermann   In any event, they do something other than what I want. During the
working process, they initially present me with a certain resistance, which I can only control up to
a certain degree. I think that the paintings do, indeed, lead their own life to a certain extent. That
becomes particularly clear when they leave the studio. When you look at the special case of "paintings
in an exhibition context", the paintings want, first and foremost, to be noticed. They compete for
perception; experience shows that what I am trying to instill in them is not necessarily the same as
what other viewers get out of it. Someone who goes to my exhibitions and sees the paintings most
likely gets something else out of it than what I tried to put into it.

M.F.   The paintings compete for perception. What sort of perception do your paintings
seek? Could it be pictured like a seismograph that searches for the fields where this perception could
be particularly successful?

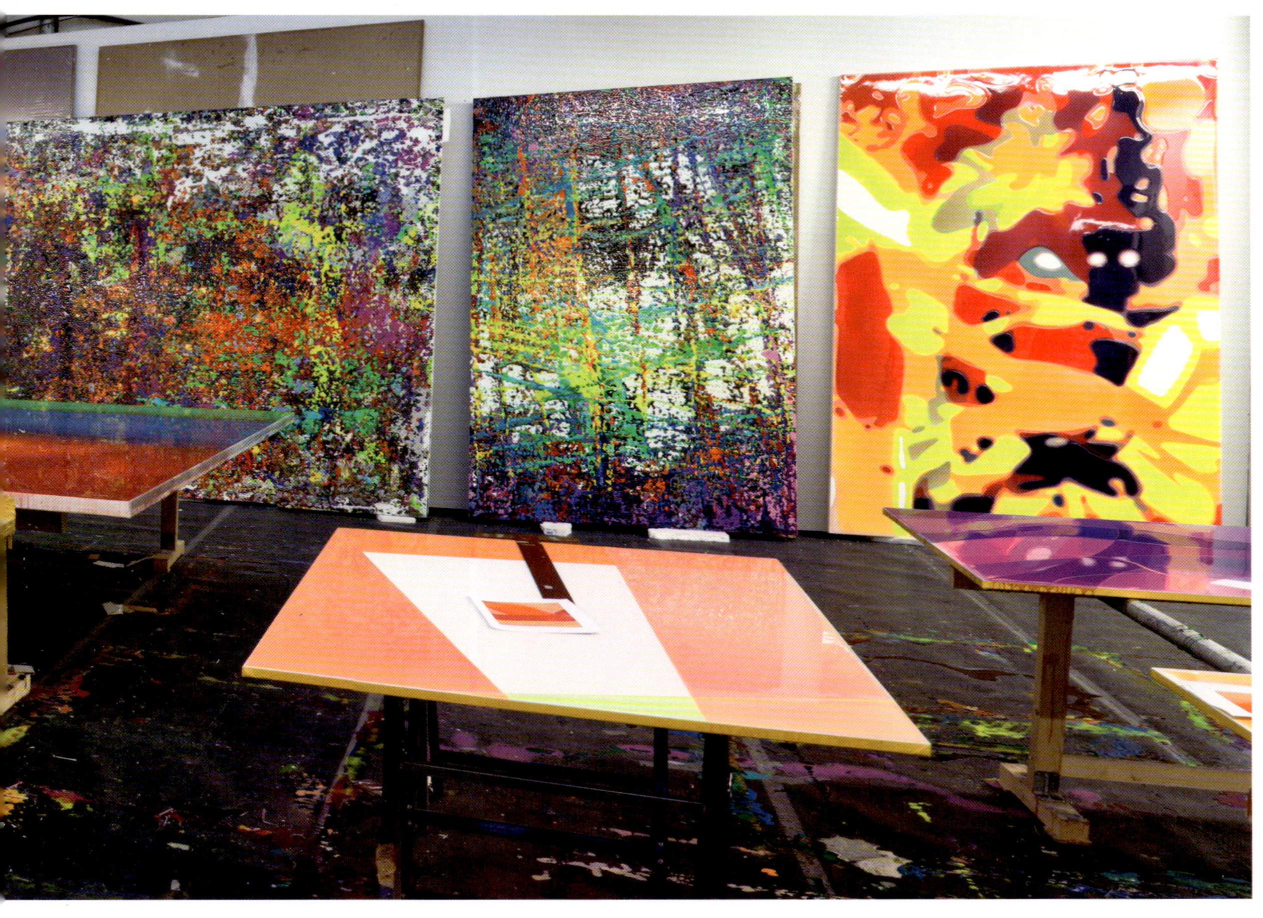

主題：爭奪感觀的繪畫、融合而非瓦解、一個畫家的奢侈

Marietta Franke　　　今天我們在你的科隆工作室會面，談論你近四年來的繪畫作品。畫作具有自己的生命。你怎麼看待「繪畫的要求」這種說法？

Peter Zimmerman　　　無論如何，作品所做到的跟我想要的并不一樣。開始創作時，作品會對我進行對抗，這是我不能完全控制的。我認為繪畫在某程度上的確擁有自己的生命。作品離開畫室後，這就變得特別明顯。在「展覽」這種特定環境中，作品最大的要求就是贏取注意，它們爭奪感觀。經驗告訴我，我試圖投入作品的東西與觀者所獲得的東西未必一致。一個人來到我的展覽，看我的畫，他的收穫極有可能出於我意料之外。

M.F.　　你說繪畫爭奪感觀。你的作品期待怎樣的感觀？它們是否像一幅地震儀圖，在探測感官反應最有效的領域？

P.Z.　　藝術是我的工作領域，所以我的作品首先應被視為藝術，但同時我亦樂於質疑感觀的真實性。當代人處處遭受視覺衝擊：火爐（那邊就有一個）、電視機、電影院、廣告版等種種事物都在爭奪我們的感觀和注意。當我的作品在展覽中可以與其他環境的圖像作出抗衡，我認為這是一種成就。

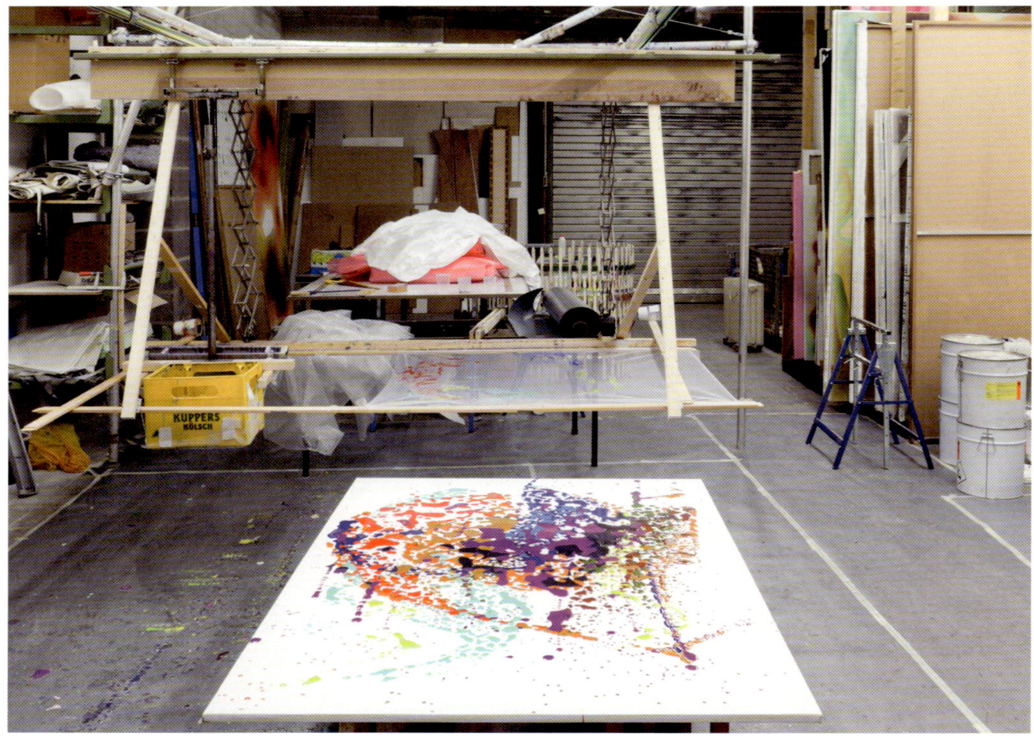

P.Z.   Since I work in the field of art, they should first and foremost be perceived as art. At the same time, I also enjoy questioning the reality of perception. What I mean is that nowadays, we are visually bombarded from all sides: open fires (there is one lit over there), TV screens, movie theaters, billboards, etc. – all of that demands our perception. When my paintings in an exhibition withstand that competition from images in other contexts, I consider that to be a quality.

M.F.   Would you like to transcend that?
P.Z.   Gladly. In principle, yes. But it is difficult to find a statement in that regard.
To transcend that can only mean to clarify the distinction from other spheres, such as film, advertising, fashion, etc.

M.F.   You use images from the media, fuse those images on your screen, making them into a kind of primordial soup, and draw new images out of it. Does the distinction between Studium and Punctum, which Roland Barthes introduced with regard to viewing photographs, play a role? I mean that an image that contains a Punctum that cannot be decoded or clarified, and therefore retains a residuum, remains an image; in contrast to that, an image that can be decoded from the Studium viewpoint is decipherable and therefore no longer an image.

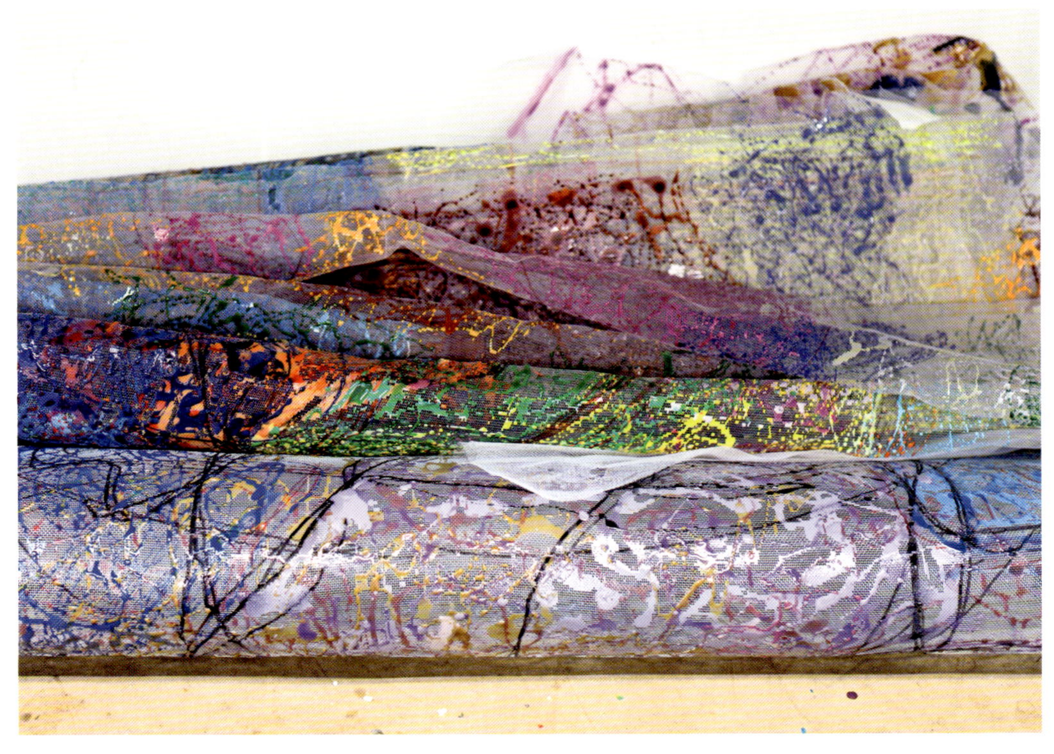

M.F.　　你希望超越這種抗衡嗎？

P.Z.　　原則上，答案是當然，但對這個問題下定論很困難。「超越」的意思不過是清楚區分電影、廣告、時裝等各種領域。

M.F.　　你挪用媒體圖像，在屏幕上把它溶合至一種原始的渾沌狀態，然後從中提煉出新圖像。這跟羅蘭・巴特討論攝影時提出的知面 (Studium) 與刺點 (Punctum) 兩個概念有沒有關係？我想說的是，擁有刺點 (Punctum) 的圖像拒絕被解碼或闡明，保留一點殘餘物，所以它仍是圖像。與之相反，圖像從知面 (Studium) 角度被完全解讀後，就不再是圖像了。

P.Z.　　我需要以一幅原始圖像作為起點，因為我不願意單憑想象或直覺創作。但我亦不希望觀者着意追溯圖像的源頭，因為這并不是享受作品的條件。我不過是留下一絲線索。從知面 (Studium) 中把刺點 (Punctum) 解脫，提取隱晦的、被湮沒的、神奇的元素，這本身已是一種樂趣。還原與重現被混淆的圖像，是一個返璞歸真的過程。在我而言，繪畫作品如何誕生的確是一個深切的問題，但我不必清楚交代創作起點。更重要的是作品的「在場」或「出現」，是它有沒有令觀眾驚歎的魅力。在這個層面上，我的想法跟巴特的概念是有相關性的。

M.F.　　你近四年的畫作中，包括所謂的「團狀畫」（Blob Painting），即以重疊光彩而成的作品，亦包括以點滴顏料堆砌而成的作品，猶如天際繁星。有些作品探索各種光暗現象，更有作品則與印象派風格幾乎同出一轍。這些繪畫可以抵擋其他圖像環境，甚至超越它們嗎？

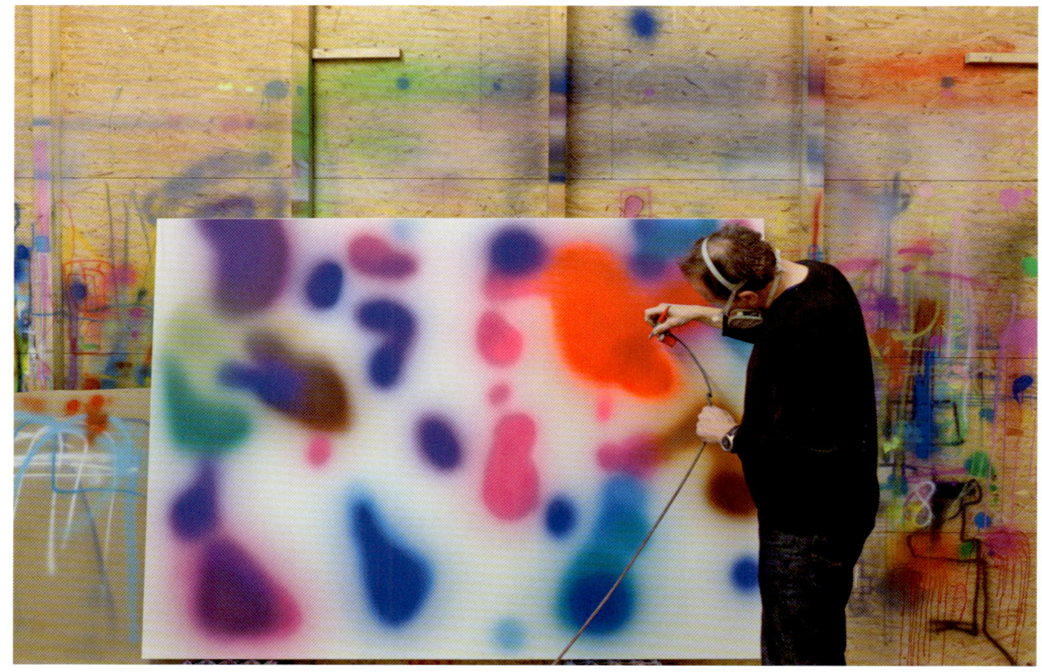

P.Z.   The original image I start out with is necessary because I do not want to come up with something or make a gut positing. In that respect, I need the original image. I do not want anyone to be able to trace it back to that particular picture. In addition, it is not critical for the enjoyment of an image. I leave a trail. The Studium from this Punctum, to practically extricate the obscure, obliterated, and mystical elements can already constitute a certain pleasure, to reverse the obfuscation process and the traces of the machine that melts down the whole thing to decipher it and make it once again visible. The story of how the paintings come to be is, indeed, important to me. However, the starting point must not necessarily be recognizable. What is important is the presence or appearance of a painting, that it has something that surprises and impresses the viewer. In that respect, there is a certain correlation to Roland Barthes' Studium and Punctum.

M.F.   Among the paintings that have come out of the last four years are the so-called Blob Paintings, or paintings with overlapping layers of light. There are paintings with piles of dots – something that can be observed in the cosmos. There are paintings that play on light / shadow or light / dark situations. And then there are the paintings that have something practically impressionistic about them. Are they paintings that can withstand these other image situations and perhaps transcend them?

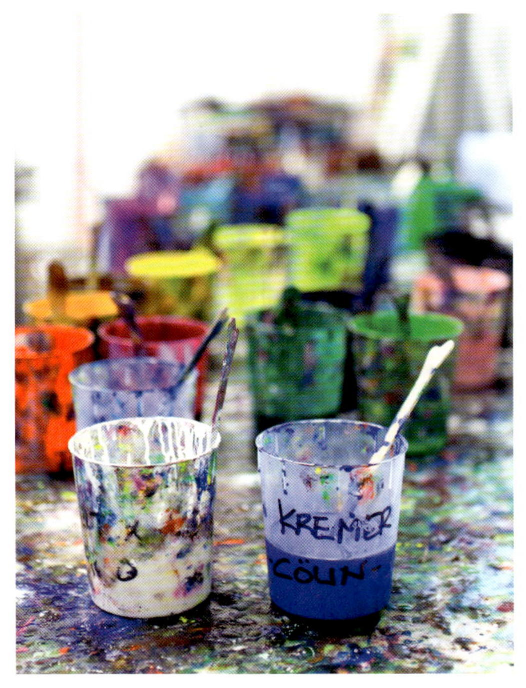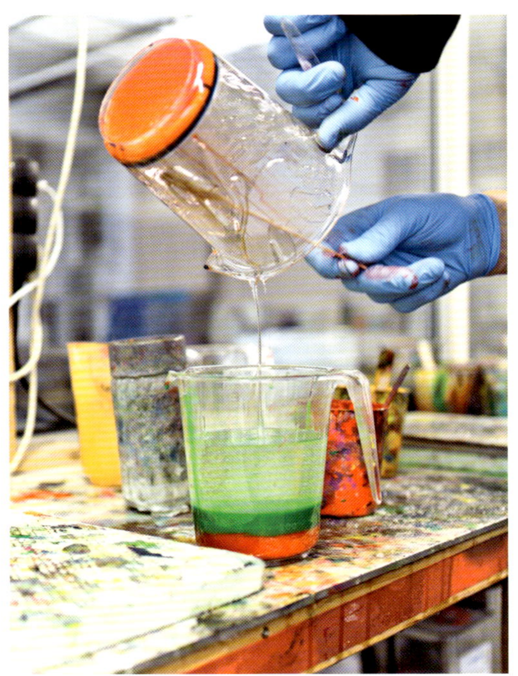

P.Z.　　最少可以說有點希望。印象主義在我的創作過程中絕對沒有主導意義。當我以觀者身份回顧作品時，才注意到印象派的影子，而這大概不外乎我對某些色彩及光暗效果的執著。再者，你不能忽視一幅畫是怎樣畫出來的。我的作品衍生自屏幕上的圖像，如何透過繪畫傳達屏幕的亮度與色度，對我非常重要。這牽涉一種時空落差，因為你畢竟不能以物質形式複製屏幕的光學效果。傳統繪畫使用的是顏料，而屏幕的圖像則由光與電所產生，是兩種不同的方法，但我力求把它們拉近。

M.F.　　你的作品容易跟射光主義、印象主義、色域繪畫等藝術浪潮扯上關係，或被草草標籤為抽象藝術。它們有着被誤解的風險。

P.Z.　　我並不排除這些誤解，甚至可能會刻意玩弄藝術史典故。也許這些典故頗切合某些展覽的主題。但我現在所運用的是一批自己搜集回來的媒體圖像，它們的創作地點及時期我都一一標明。一幅描繪屏幕的畫作導致誤解，也許因為傳統繪畫素材不能逼真地重現電子影像。

M.F.　　你覺得科技性的感官刺激是否比傳統藝術優越？

P.Z.　　是的。你留意過手提電話、屏幕等媒體對孩子們的刺激後，會發現繪畫很難與之相比。

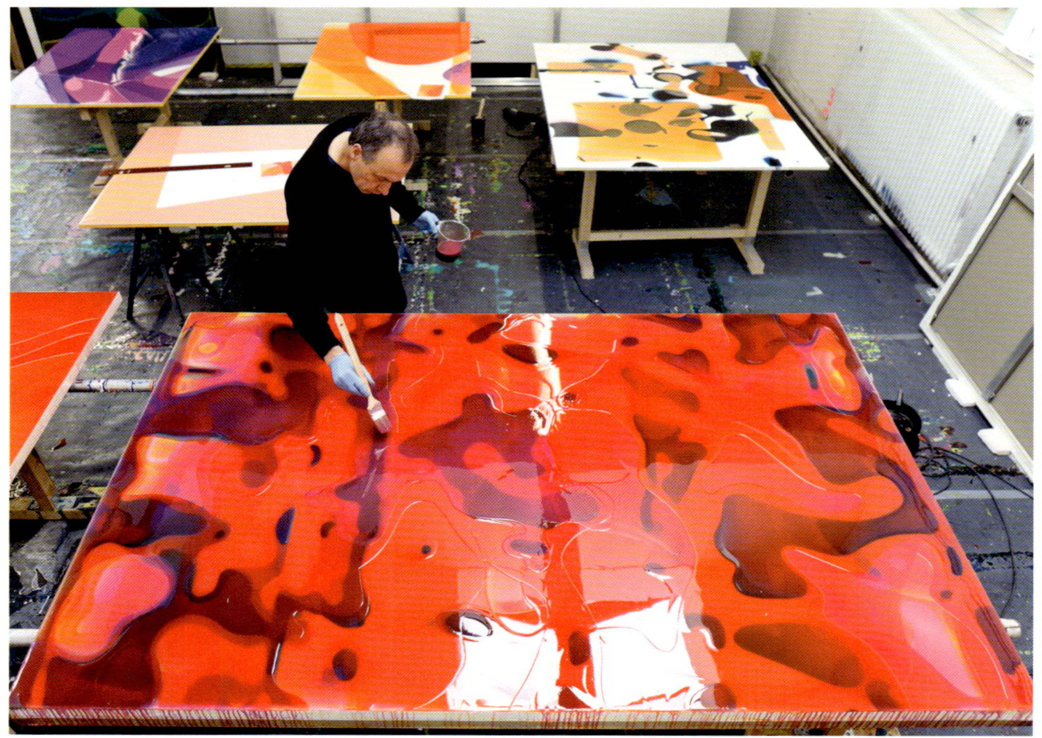

P.Z.   In the very least, there is a certain hope associated with it. – When creating, Impressionism is certainly not a category that brings me to achieve a certain result. In hindsight, if I put myself in the shoes of the viewer, impressionistic aspects could be present in it. Perhaps simply due to the fact that I value a certain color effect and light situation. In addition, you have to get into the issue of how such a painting is created. My paintings are based on models that are taken from the screen. It is important to me that the luminosity and color intensity on the screen also be conveyed in the painted image. Therein lies a certain anachronism, because you cannot transfer the colors generated on the screen to an image that is painted with colored matter. When you paint an image in the traditional sense, you must do so with color pigments, whereas they are generated by light and electricity on the screen. In that respect, the methods are different, but I try to get as close as I can to the same effect.

M.F.   Your paintings may run the risk of being associated with movements that have taken place in the history of art, such as Rayonism, Impressionism or Color Field Painting, or they will simply be classified as abstract art. You are exposing them to the possibility of being misunderstood.

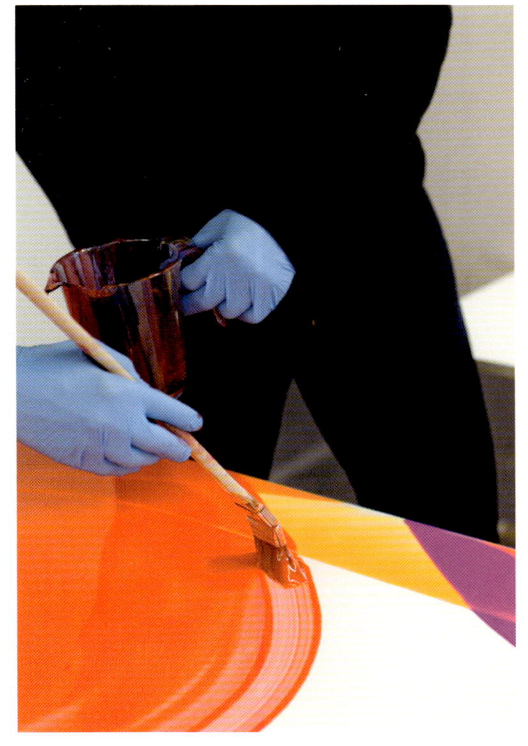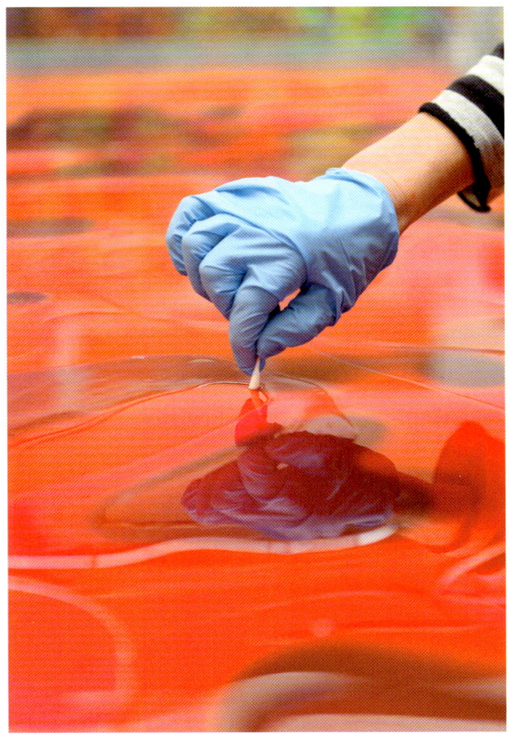

M.F.　所以你追求一種直接的震撼，先把觀者抓住，不留他反思的空間。

P.Z.　對。

M.F.　你經常從觀者的角度思考。當他被作品抓住，他必須繼續面對整件作品。這個理想的觀者會這麼做？

P.Z.　沒有所謂理想的觀者。你必須假定畫家與觀者的動機有一種基本區別，亦應該記住語言、溝通系統的種種偶然性。早期的我對這種張力特別感興趣，在數件作品中探索過這些問題：圖像都是能讀清楚的文本嗎？抑或包含直覺與感情、以及難以言喻、無法傳達的東西？

M.F.　你現在說的是過往的情況。例如，1994至1995年間你曾製作過一些海報，仿佛朝著某種想法或意念發展，但并沒有完工。你是否有意捉弄及挑戰觀者，從而使他發現藝術中不可言喻的部分？

P.Z.　我們的做法是把文字投射到海報上，排版佈局使個別字詞成為亮點。用心細讀的觀者可以把整段文字像故事般讀懂。明亮的字詞本身並沒有任何意義，它們的作用不過是阻礙理解。理解并不是作品的目的，不然我會把文字直接打印在A4紙上。

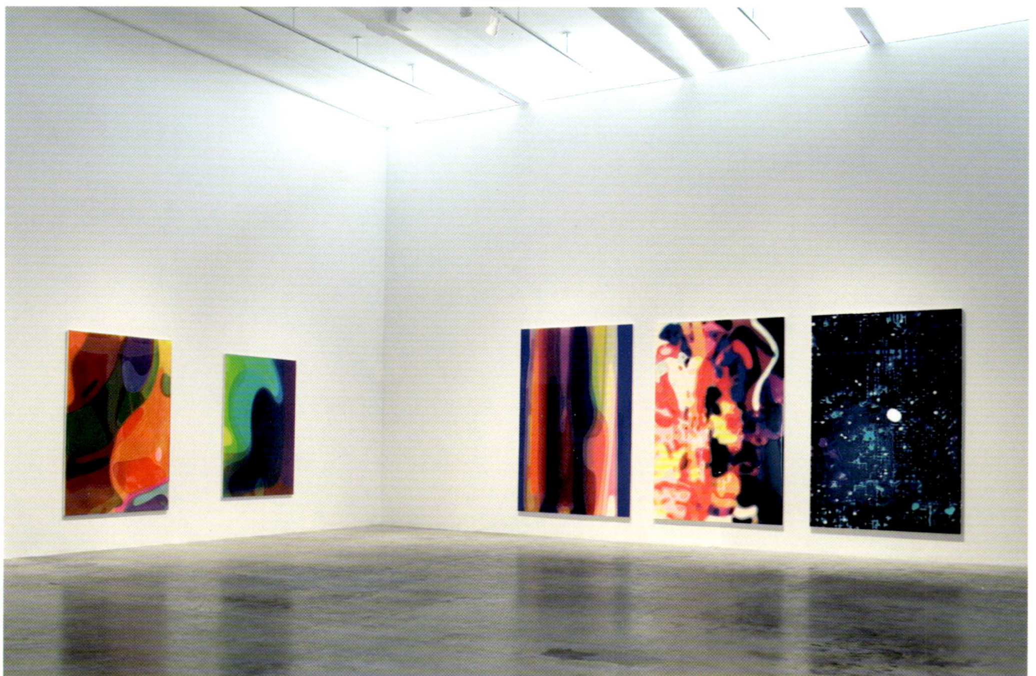

P.Z.   Such misunderstandings cannot be ruled out. I may also play with these cross references. It is possible that such references lend themselves well to certain exhibitions. But I now rely on an independent repertoire of found images that makes it clear where these images are from and when they were created. When representing (screen) light, for example, the misunderstanding may come from the fact that a technical image cannot be honored or sufficiently implemented with conventional painting materials.

M.F.   Do you see these technical possibilities as superior?

P.Z.   I think so. When you watch, for example, how children respond to a key media stimulus, a cell phone or a screen, it is not so simple for a painting to compete with that.

M.F.   So you rely on an immediate effect that the viewer cannot at first reconsider, into which he simply enters, that grabs him.

P.Z.   That is correct.

M.F.   You think a lot in the direction of the viewer; when he has been grabbed, he must continue to deal with the whole thing. What does this viewer who responds ideally to your works do?

"mazed" 2012
Epoxy resin on canvas
250 x 160 cm / 8.2 feet x 63 inches

迷惘 2012年
環氧樹脂帆布畫
250 x 160公分 / 8.2英呎 x 63英吋

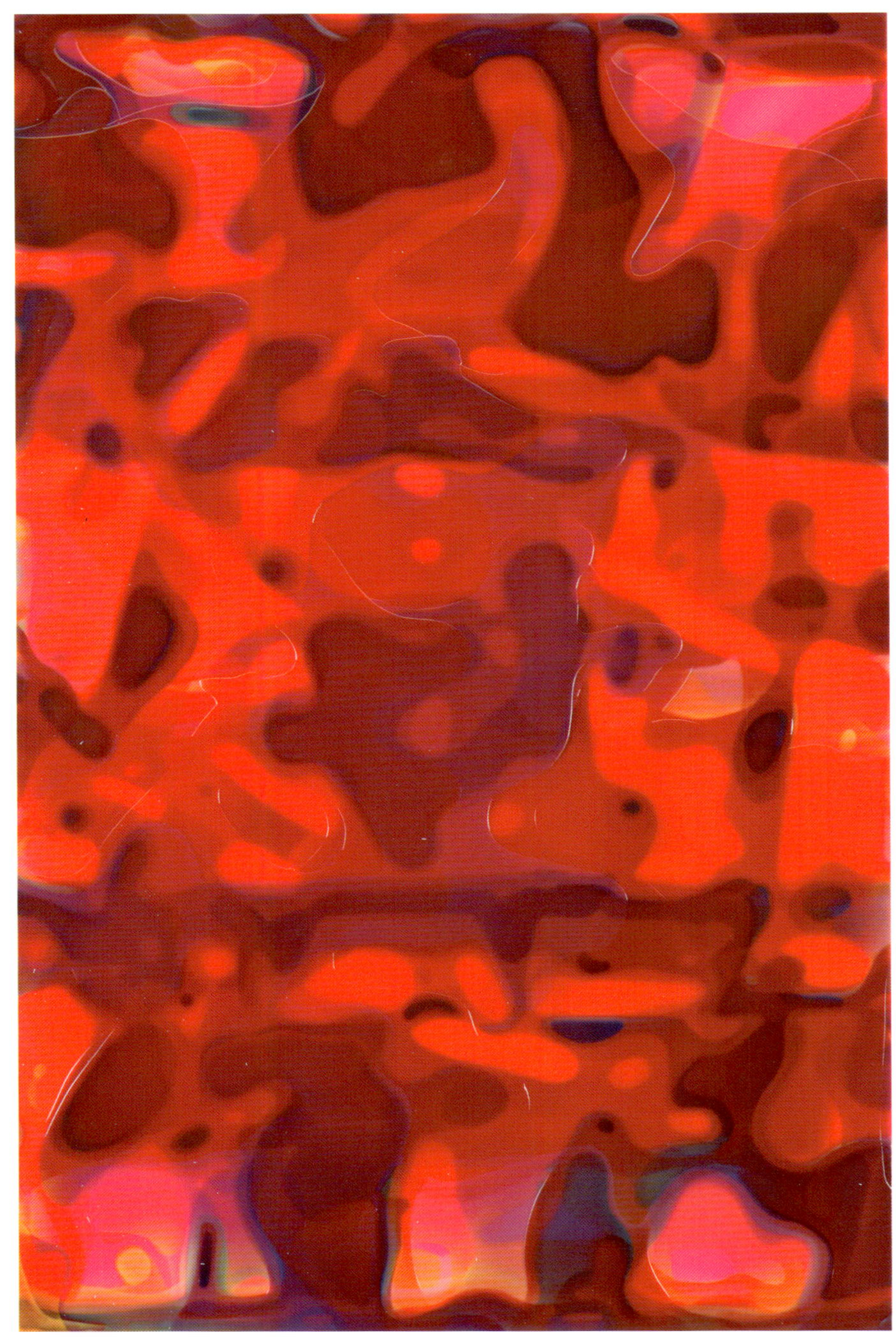

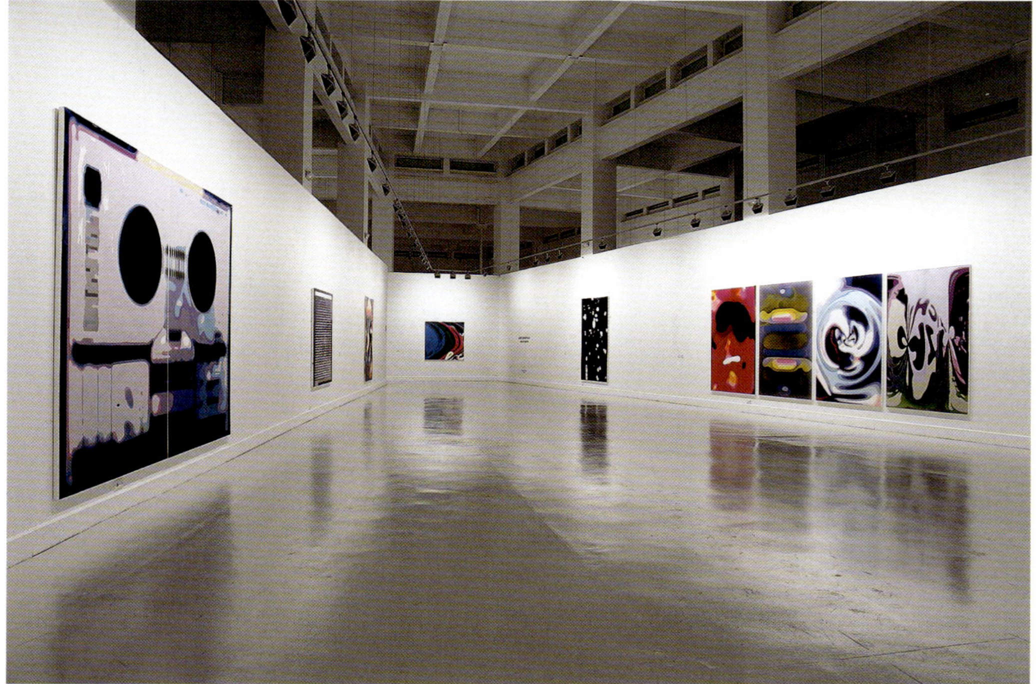

P.Z.   There is no ideal viewer. I think you must presume there is a basic difference of interest between the painter and the viewer. And, of course, you must also bear in mind the contingent language or communication patterns. In my early work, I was particularly interested in that tension, and at that time, I addressed it in several works. The following question in particular preoccupied me: are images texts that can be read clearly? Or is there a certain a lack of definition that takes place on an intuitive, nonverbal, also emotional level that cannot be communicated?

M.F.   You are now speaking of previous situations. For example, you made posters (1994-1995) that apparently went in a certain direction, with regard to sense or ideas, but then cut their expression short. Was it intended to tease the viewer, incite or provoke him in order to thrust him into the unsayable aspect of art?

P.Z.   With the posters, we have a coherent text projected on found posters. Certain terms are highlighted depending on where they appear in the layout. Whoever lets himself sink into this work could, with a certain amount of effort, understand the text, like a continuous text, a little story. The highlighted terms have, in and of themselves, no meaning and provoke a certain lack of understanding. But if they were about readability, I would have printed the text on a sheet of A4 paper.

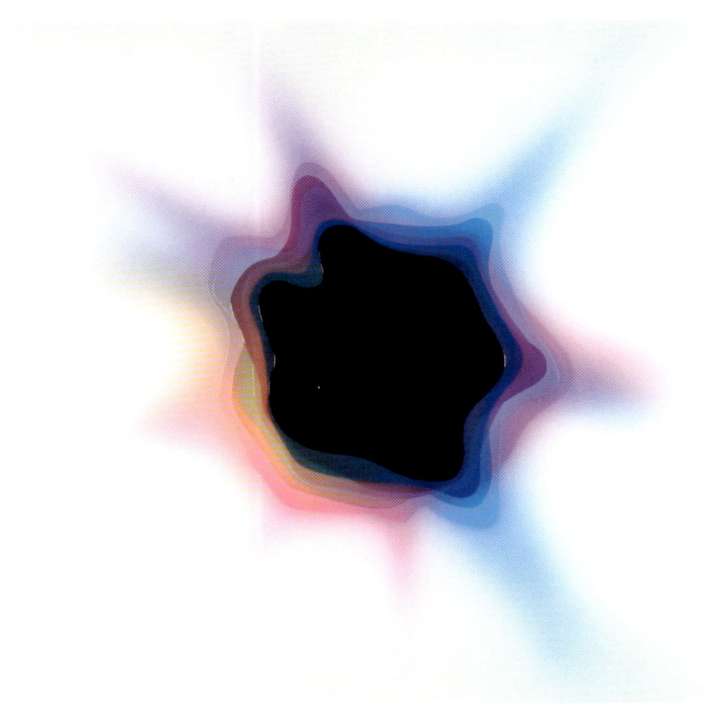

M.F.　　這樣擾亂了觀者的感觀習慣，可能也使他們感到不安。

P.Z.　　海報作品令我懊惱的地方，是很多人根本沒有留心看，只以為它是一張普通海報，唯有在提醒之下才發現它異常之處。我的意圖的確是擾亂感觀與營造不安感。這裏我探討的問題是：在甚麼條件之下某些主題能變成藝術？

M.F.　　你可能透過藝術肯定了「世界缺乏被觀察的可能性」這個說法（尼克拉斯‧盧曼）。

P.Z.　　那是關於世上種種盲點的說法。我感興趣的問題反而是：究竟在甚麼條件或系統得到滿足之後，一幅信息不一的海報才可保持整體性，而不至於瓦解？怎麼可以把互相抵觸、甚至互相矛盾的意義集合成一個個體，而避免淪落至混亂無序的狀態？文字覆蓋整張海報，正在處理這個現象。

M.F.　　要言之，融合勝於瓦解。你探索過圖像變成文字的狀態，然後放下了這個想法。後來（1999至2000年間）你開始對圖像作為圖像的本質感興趣，作品中隨之突顯出一種純繪畫性。抽象、非物體的圖像是不是回歸圖像本質的途徑？

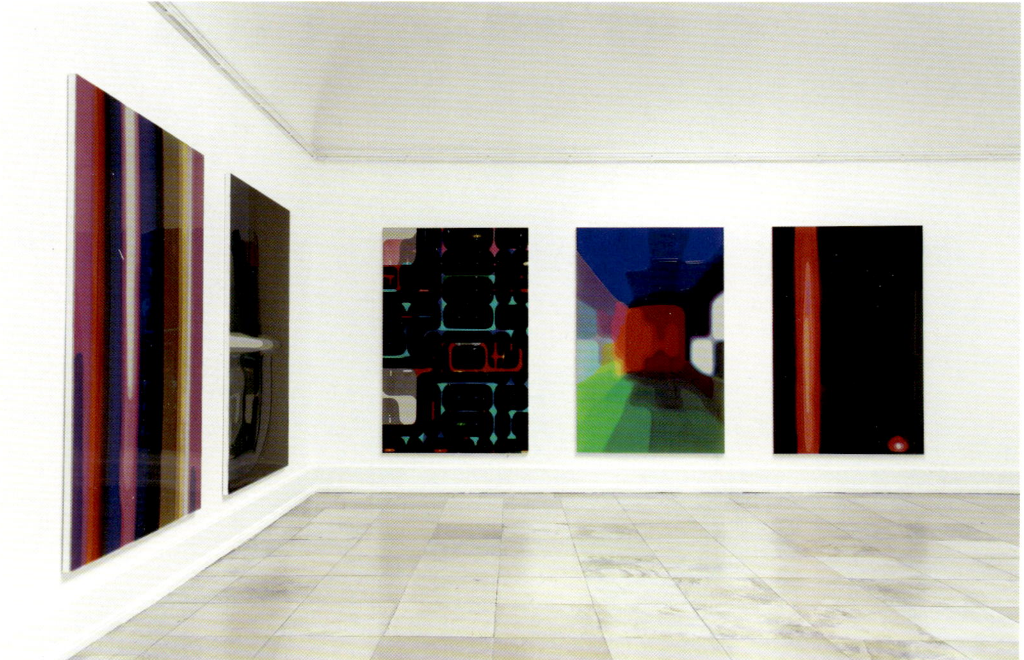

M.F.   Habits of perception were disrupted. Perhaps interferences and uncertainty.

P.Z.   What was irritating about this poster work was that a lot of people never even discovered this work and took it 1:1. Only when it had been pointed out to them did they realize that there was something different there. In that respect, this disruption effect or uneasiness was an intended positing. For me, it was a study of under which conditions certain subjects become art.

M.F.   It could be an artistic form of the admission of "lack of observability of the world" (Niklas Luhmann).

P.Z.   That is in reference to the blind spots of the world. For me, the question is rather: What conditions or structures must be fulfilled so the different conclusions that represent the individual posters do not demolish the framework and make the whole thing disintegrate into single parts. What interested me, also figuratively, was how different, contradictory parts or statements are held together without falling into disorder or randomness. The text, which extends over the entire poster, deals with exactly that phenomenon.

"page" 2012
Acrylic and epoxy resin on canvas
200 x 300 cm / 6.6 x 9.1 feet

頁 2012年
環氧樹脂帆布畫
200 x 300公分 / 6.6 x 9.1英呎

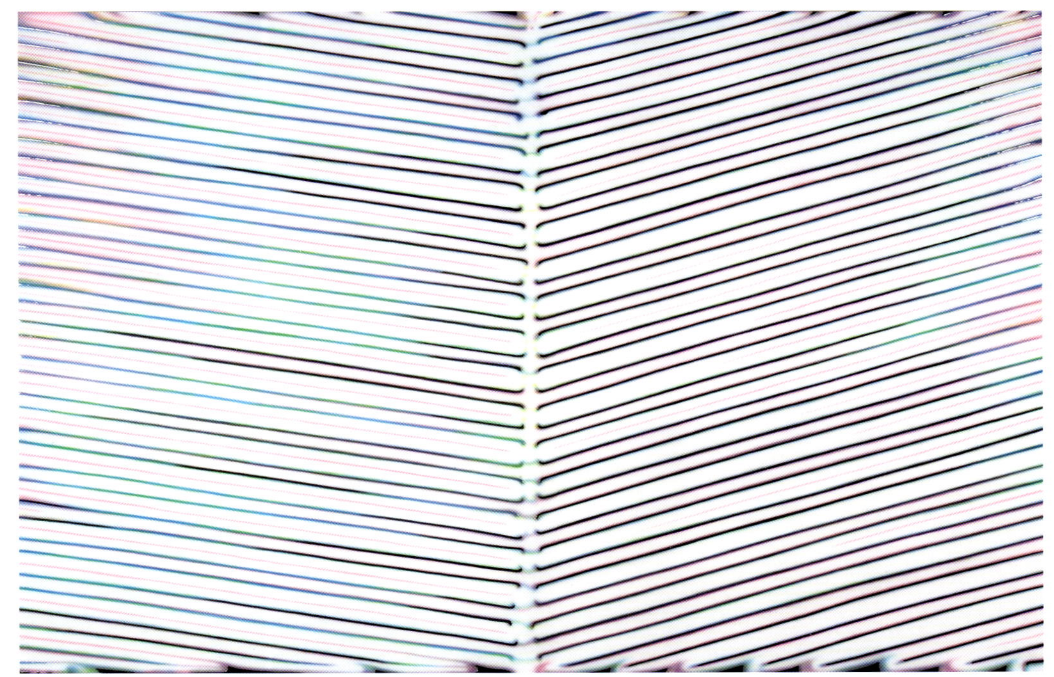

P.Z.　　我認為美好的圖像不一定是抽象的。我創作抽象作品，是因為我對圖像與文字之間的關係感興趣。電腦給了我機會以繪畫形式繼續創作，因為我可在繪畫中將圖像以文字編碼。我作品的抽象性基於意義模糊及缺乏定義，創作過程是它們有意思之地方。要處理圖像作為圖像的本質這個問題，一定要把繪畫看成一個系統，然後從系統中挑出個別圖像作評估與比較。這是一個有趣的遊戲，也花了我不少時間。我自然地會在作品中加入某些細節，表明我的創作範圍與我參照的其他繪畫定位。

M.F.　　其中包括美國繪畫。

P.Z.　　這些年來我偏好有所改變，但某些美國繪畫定位的確特別吸引我，比如莫利斯・路易斯、傑克遜・波洛克、保羅・貞金斯、及菲利普・古斯頓。我對他們的繪畫構思方式很感興趣，我也曾經把他們的作品當作模型。我在書本題目時期（1987-1999），就曾跟波洛克作出過對話。

M.F.　　你的作品包括所謂「美式」的大型格式，也有較小型的，如書本題目作品。

P.Z.　　我很希望只畫大型作品，他們的顏色與反光表面可以震撼觀者的心靈。我的媒體（環氧樹脂）比較適合大型畫面，因為它能充分反映周邊的人、物、甚至空間。大型作品更加引人入勝。當然，展覽場地是有限制的。

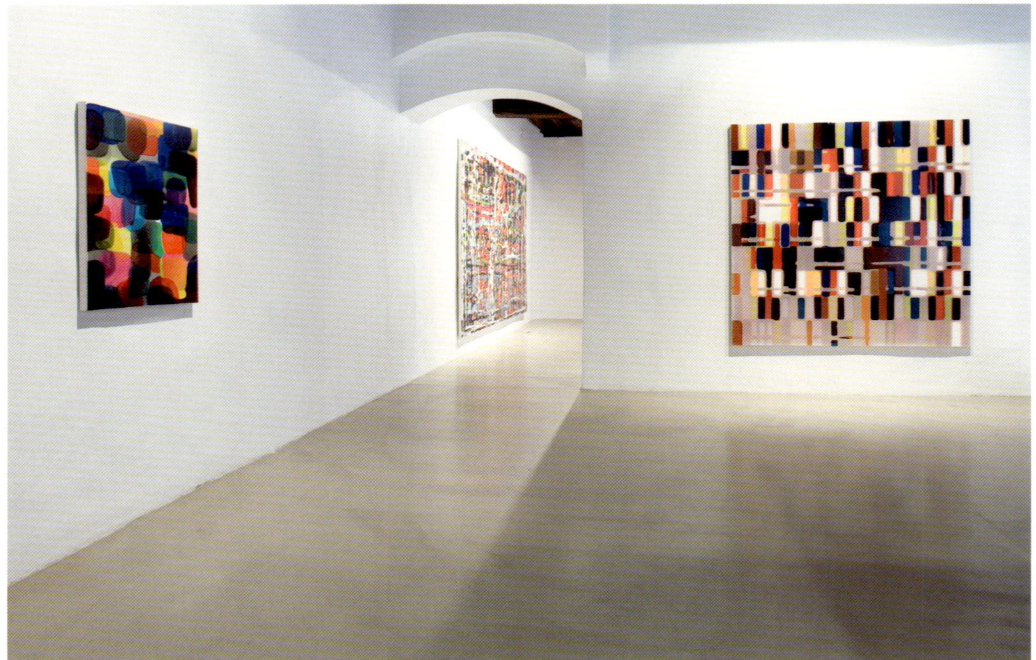

M.F.　So cohesion rather than fragmentation. You explored the idea that an image can be text, brought it to a certain point, and then left it to stand there. Later (1999-2000), you then also became interested in other issues when the question of an image as an image and painterly possibilities came to the fore. Could the abstract, i.e. nonobjective, image be a catalyst for the process of recovering the image as an image?

P.Z.　For me, an image does not necessarily have to be abstract in order to be a good image. The fact that my paintings are abstract is due to my interest in pursuing the relationship between images and text. When the computer came into play, I had the opportunity to continue my artistic work by painting because, in paintings, each image is encoded as text. My paintings are abstract because of the lack of definition and ambiguity; the way they are made makes the paintings interesting. Image as an image – that question can only be dealt with if you take painting as a system and evaluate or compare a certain image with another from that system. It is a nice game on which I spend a lot of time. I naturally try to fabricate certain details in order to show in which sphere I work, in some cross reference to other painter positions.

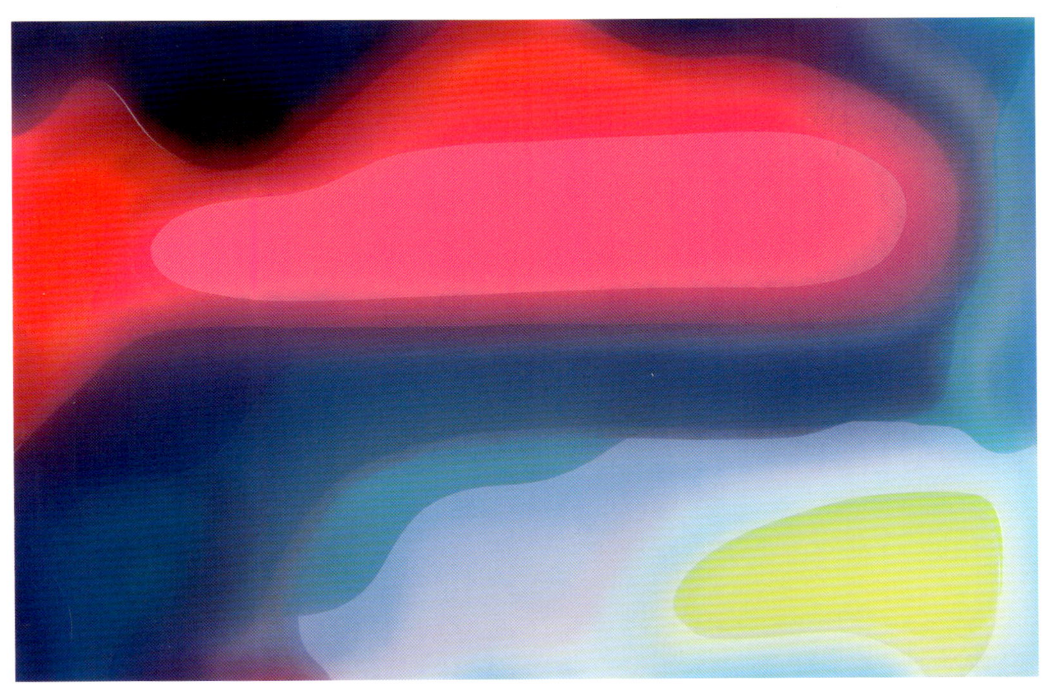

M.F.　你是一位愛探險的藝術家，勇於探索未知的事物。你並不知道終點是甚麼。

P.Z.　以前的我更是這樣。現在我感覺我的活動空間縮小了，因為每一件新作品都撤除了某些可能性。

M.F.　我留意到你在談話中發展新思路。

P.Z.　可能現在我更讓自己以畫家身份說話。

M.F.　但你說話時還是保留了藝術思考的概念性。

P.Z.　是的。補充說一句，我所謂的「畫家身份」是指一種奢侈，一種隱藏特定藝術可能性而專注於繪畫問題的自由。

M.F.　是一種自我克制，迫使自己靠近圖像作為圖像的本質？

P.Z.　儘管我明白純粹的圖像是不存在的。

M.F.　它是一個構思，正如「作為文字的圖像」是一個構思。

P.Z.　我當然意識到創作背後的概念和語境。但是，當我們實實在在地探討一張圖像的好壞、它的轉換可能性、如何將它一筆一劃地畫在畫布上等問題時，理論性的考慮都是次要的。

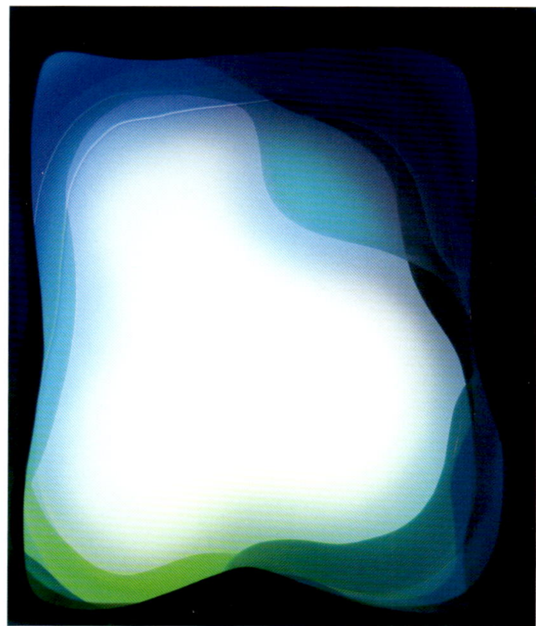

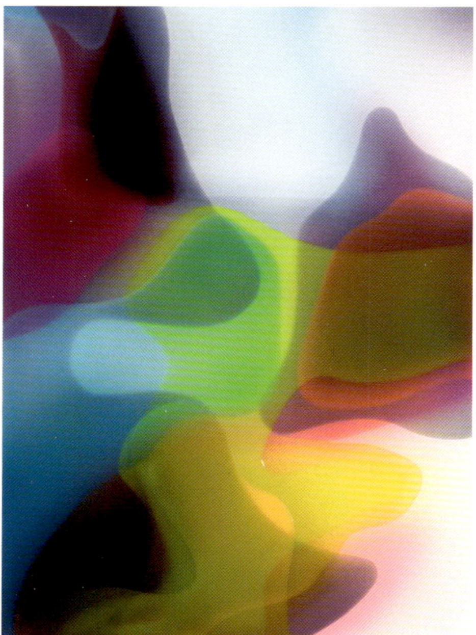

M.F.   Among which, there are also references to American painting.

P.Z.   I have certain preferences that have changed with the years. But it is certainly true that certain painter positions from American painting are of particular interest to me. These include Morris Louis, Jackson Pollock, but also Paul Jenkins and Phillip Guston. I am interested in their conceptual approach to painting. For example, I have used some of those artists' paintings as models. I dealt with Jackson Pollock in my book title phase (1987-1999).

M.F.   You use large, so-called American formats, but you are also familiar with small formats, like your paintings that deal with book titles.

P.Z.   I wish I could just make large paintings. With large paintings, there is the fact that you can stand in front of them and be overwhelmed by a color and a reflective surface. The experience of standing in front of such a big painting is more striking. Of course, showrooms do have certain limits.

M.F.   You are an artist who is strongly driven to explore things, to get into the unknown, to investigate. You have no idea where this whole thing will lead.

P.Z.   Earlier, that was certainly even more so the case than it is now. I think that the range of motion is narrower with each new work because each new work excludes certain possibilities.

"cine" 2012
Acrylic and epoxy resin on canvas
250 x 160 cm / 8.2 feet x 63 inches

電影 2012年
環氧樹脂帆布畫
250 x 160公分 / 8.2英呎 x 63英吋

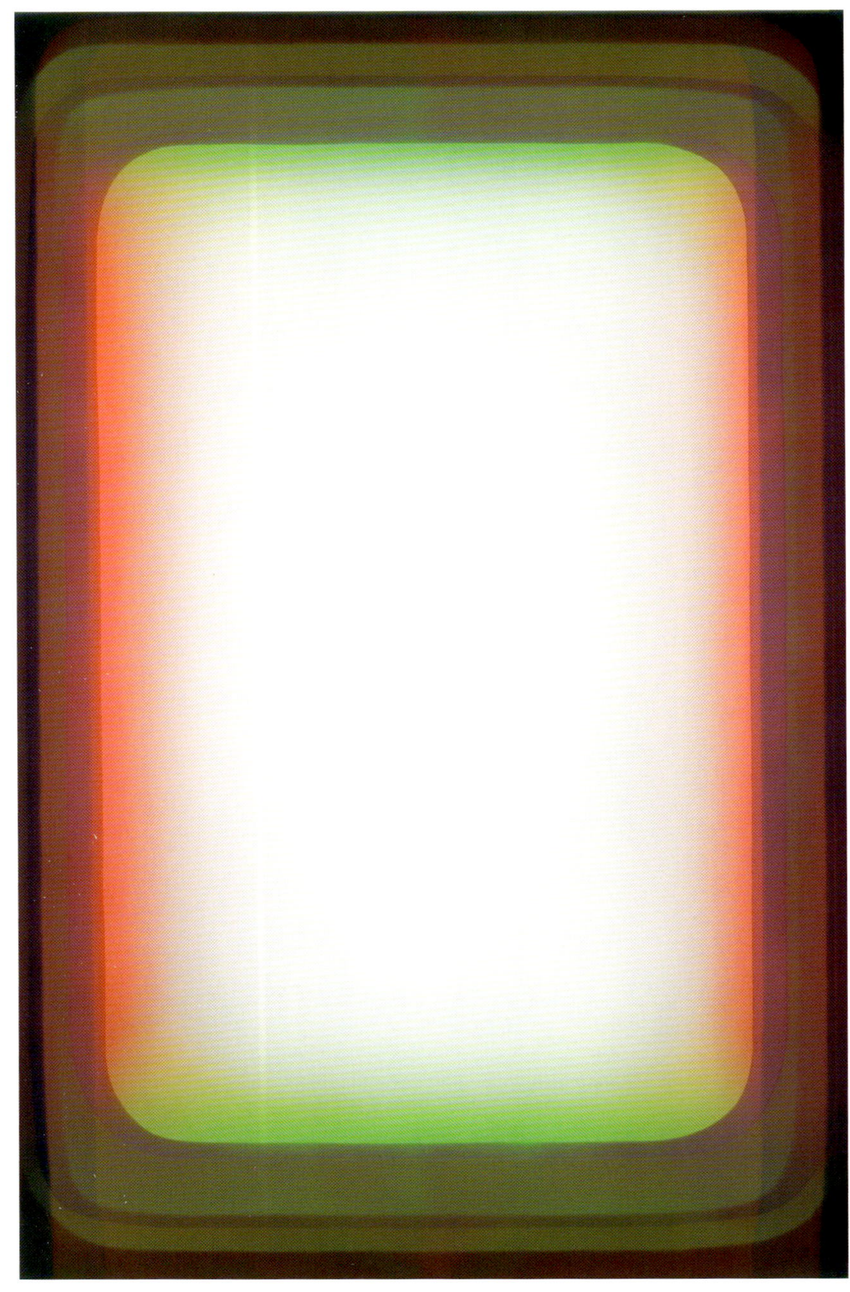

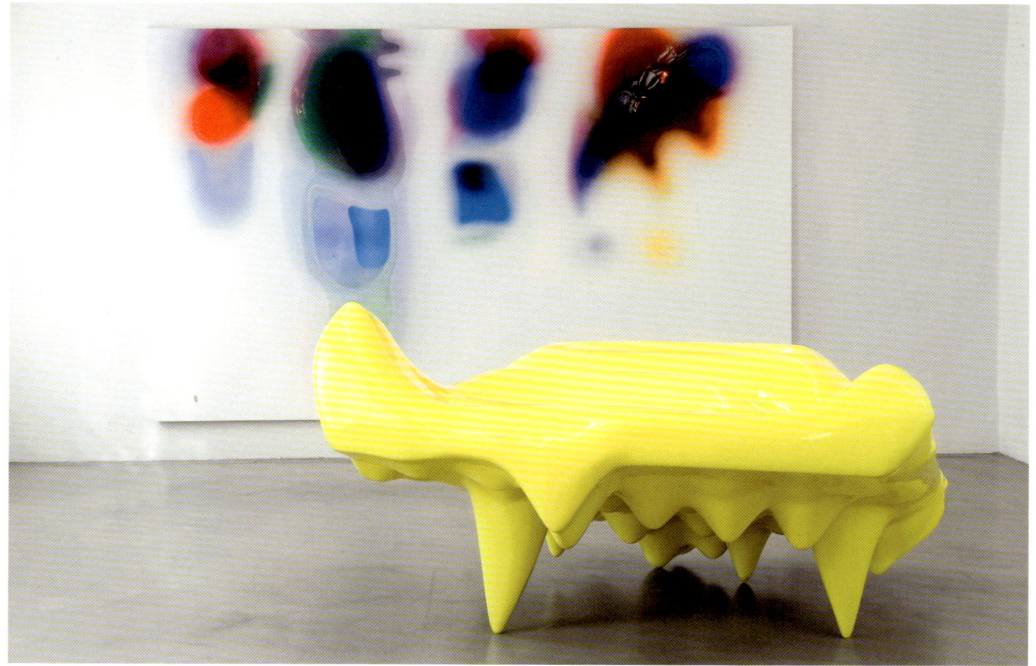

M.F.   I notice that you develop ideas while talking.
P.Z.   Perhaps I am now allowing myself to speak more from a painter position.

M.F.   The conceptual linking of your artistic thinking remains.
P.Z.   It remains. I could add that what is meant by the painter's position is the luxury to hide very specific artistic opportunities and to focus on painterly issues.

M.F.   Self-restraint in order to potentially get closer to the image as an image?
P.Z.   But I also understand that an image as an image does not exist.

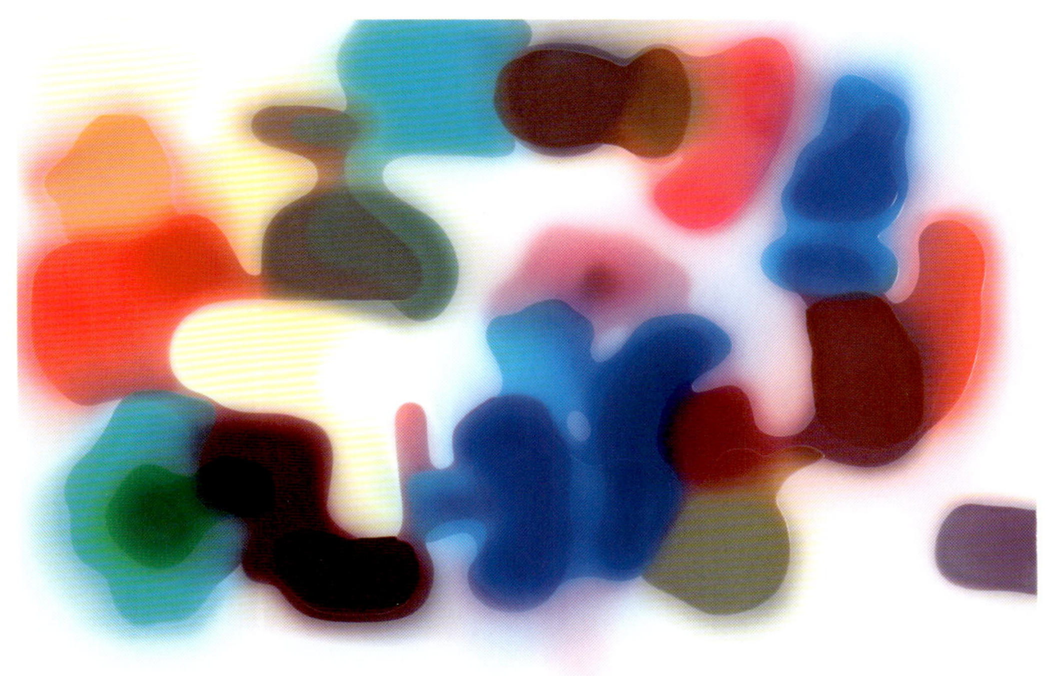

M.F.　　無容置疑，你的作品在形式上是多元和異質的。這跟藝術是無法形容、無法擁有這個現實有沒有關係？繪畫是否永遠在觸摸之外？

P.Z.　　剛才我們提到，畫作具有自己的生命。創作時靈機一觸，突然找到新出路的感覺，依然令我興奮。這種經驗往往發自構思之外，無法預測，但它會為作品帶來突破，是難能可貴的。不過，我們大部分時間還是刻意發展自己既定的範圍。古今藝術史大概就是受這種地盤戰所左右，但它的動機往往是傲慢和自大的。

M.F.　　那麼，地盤戰中你的敵人是誰？換言之，當你面對着如格哈特‧里希特的作品時，你有甚麼想法？當代的繪畫可以是甚麼？里希特的作品從多方面試圖回答這個問題，但沒有給予我們一個答案。問題依舊存在。

P.Z.　　我十分同意他的立場，大概因為他把問題留空。我自己也沒法解答這個問題，並且懷疑裝作有答案的人。

M.F.　　瓦西裡‧康定斯基下了不少功夫，提出「藝術中的精神」理論，以求賦予他的抽象藝術一種獨特的現實。你有意思限制媒體圖像的流動嗎？

P.Z.　　這是一個有趣的遊戲。

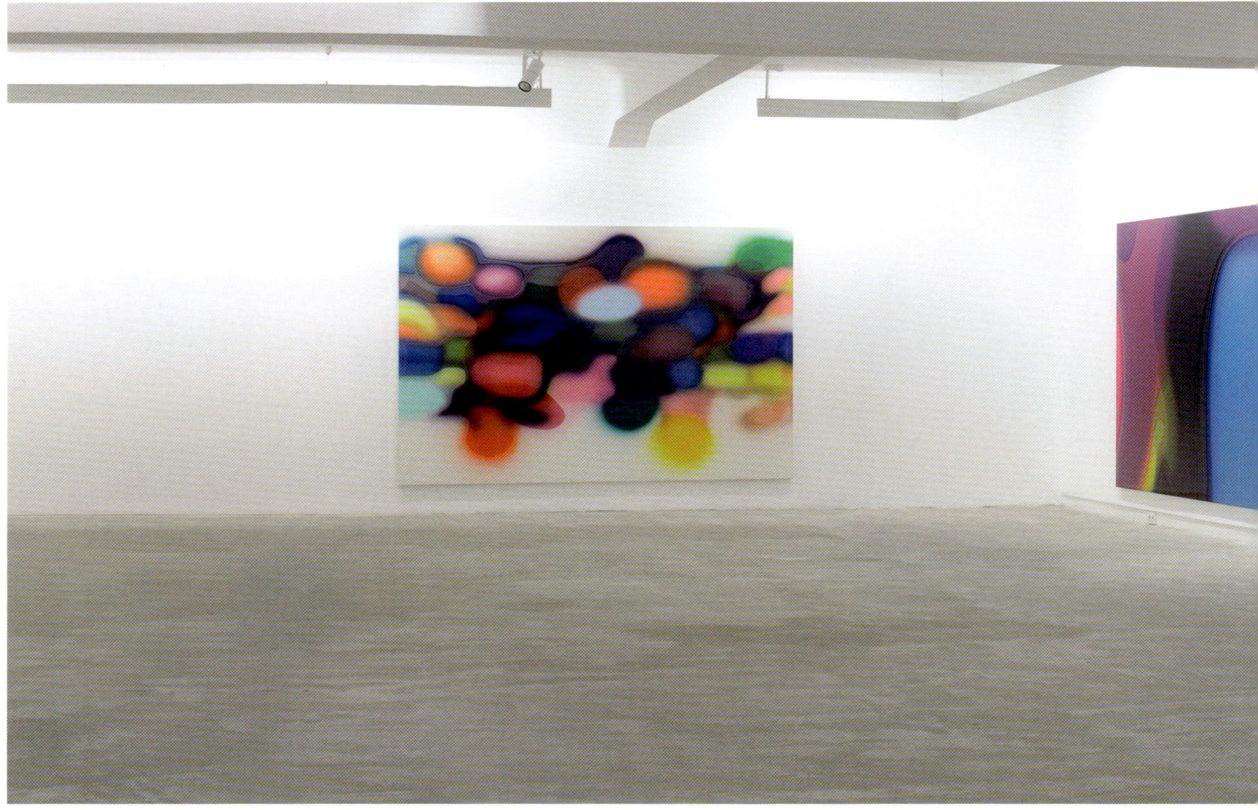

M.F.   It is a construct, just like image as text is a construct.

P.Z.   Of course I am aware of the conceptual and contextual implications. Nevertheless, in the actual practice of finding out what a good image is, how it can be transferred, and which paint maneuvers are necessary to achieve that image, theoretical considerations play a secondary role.

M.F.   The formal heterogeneity of your artistic work cannot be argued away – could it be related to the fact that art or painting cannot be described and therefore not possessed? Thus painting is somehow inapprehensible?

P.Z.   Once again, this is similar to what we said earlier about how the paintings lead their own life. It is still very exciting when suddenly, despite every system, a door opens and something unexpected happens. Its emergence, which could not have been anticipated but which advances the work, is a great moment, a great gift.

Most of the time, though, we try to conquer and cultivate a particular territory. I think recent and ancient art history is influenced by these turf wars. At the same time, though, there is a certain hubris in that.

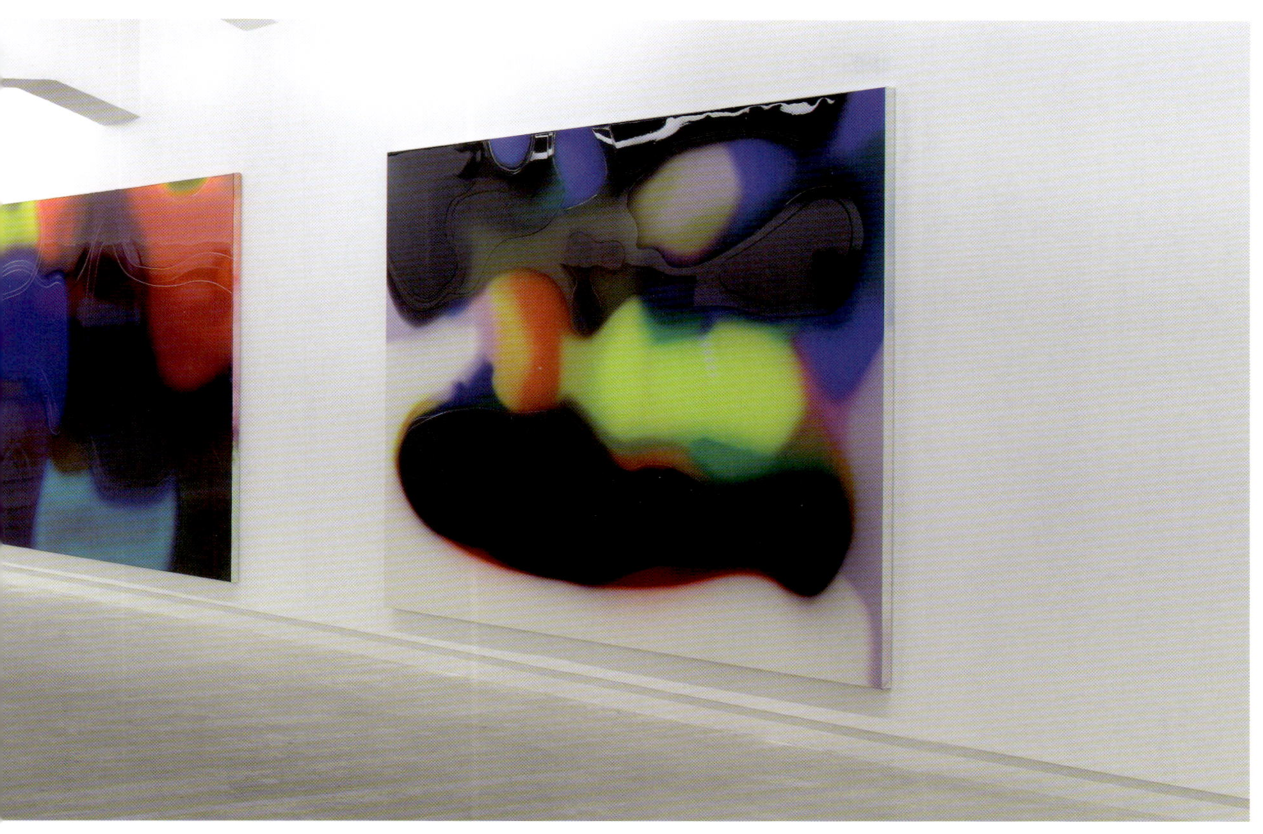

M.F.　　你認為它是一個思想遊戲。
P.Z.　　我把它看成尊重圖像的藉口。說到底，我是作品的第一位觀者。我嘗試從中尋找一點快樂、一點刺激、一個付諸行動的理由，但我不敢設想作品對其他人的意義。

M.F.　　那麼你的繪畫能算遙不可及嗎？
P.Z.　　不，代價太高了。我已經把太多的生命放在繪畫裏面，付出了實實在在的勞力和時間。這種付出固然是我個人的義務，但它在藝術史或當代社會種有沒有更廣汎的意義？這又是另外一個問題。

M.F.　　藝術可以促進世界交流嗎？
P.Z.　　藝術家永遠處於對話狀態。也許你在工作室裏埋頭畫畫，但當你展出作品時，你就在跟觀眾對話。

M.F.　　格哈特·里希特在他早年的筆記中寫道：「現在神父或哲學家已不存在，藝術家是世上最重要的人。」你覺得藝術家這麼重要嗎？
P.Z.　　我的意見比較保守。科學家、醫生、教師的重要性難道要比藝術家低嗎？你可以進一步推問：一個露宿街頭的人就微不足道嗎？創意並不是某些行業的專利，這也是顯而易見的。

M.F.　　人類能夠生活在一起，須要滿足很多不同的職責。
P.Z.　　蟻群中不只有蟻后，更有工蟻和雄蟻。分類是它們生存的最終保證。

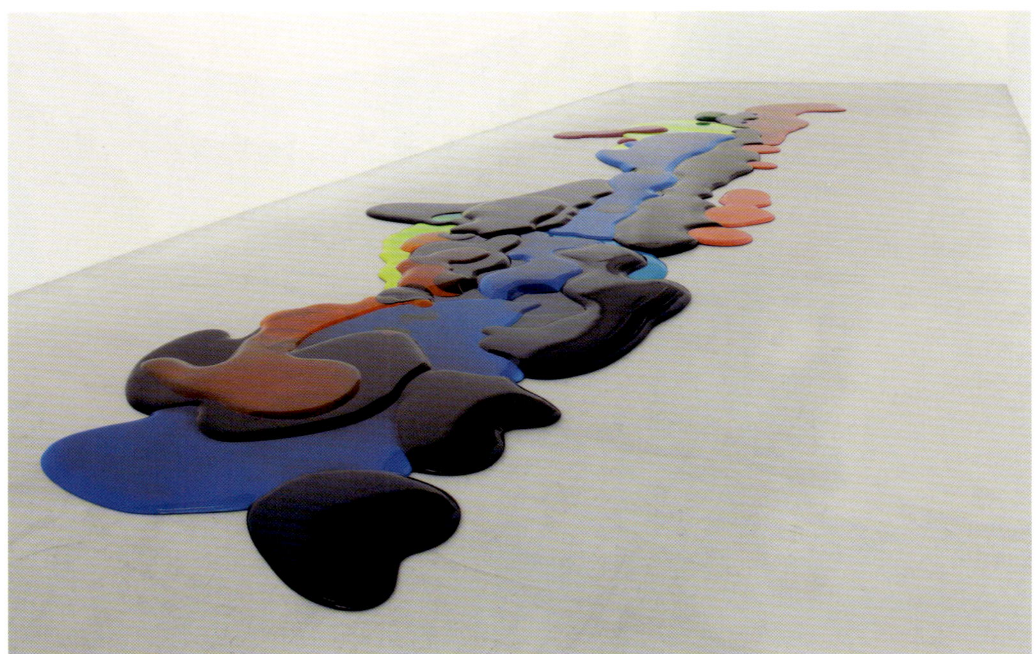

M.F.   That naturally raises the question of with whom you are waging a turf war. I can also ask the question another way: What do you think when you confront an artistic work like one by Gerhard Richter with its highly-differentiated atlas-like involvement with the question of what painting could be today – to which he also does not have an answer. The question remains.

P.Z.   I am very sympathetic to his position, probably due to the fact that he has left the question open. I cannot answer the question either. I find positions that act as if they could answer the question suspect.

M.F.   Intellectual effort like Wassily Kandinsky undertook, for example, in order to give abstract art its own reality, his entire thought on "the Spiritual in Art" – does somehow delimiting the media flow of images interest you at all?

P.Z.   It's a nice game.

M.F.   You see it as a mental game.

P.Z.   I use it as a pretext to honor it in one image or another. Ultimately, I am the first viewer of my images and I try to draw some amusement from it, to be provoked, and to be incited to some action, but I would not be so presumptuous as to think that it might be true for others.

"stains 309" 2010
Epoxy resin on rigid foam
Sitespecific work for the District Court of Düsseldorf, Germany
1400 x 700 cm / 6.6 x 9.1 feet

斑點309 2010年
環氧樹脂于硬質泡沫上 杜塞爾多夫地方法院特定作品
1400 x 700公分 / 6.6 x 9.1英呎

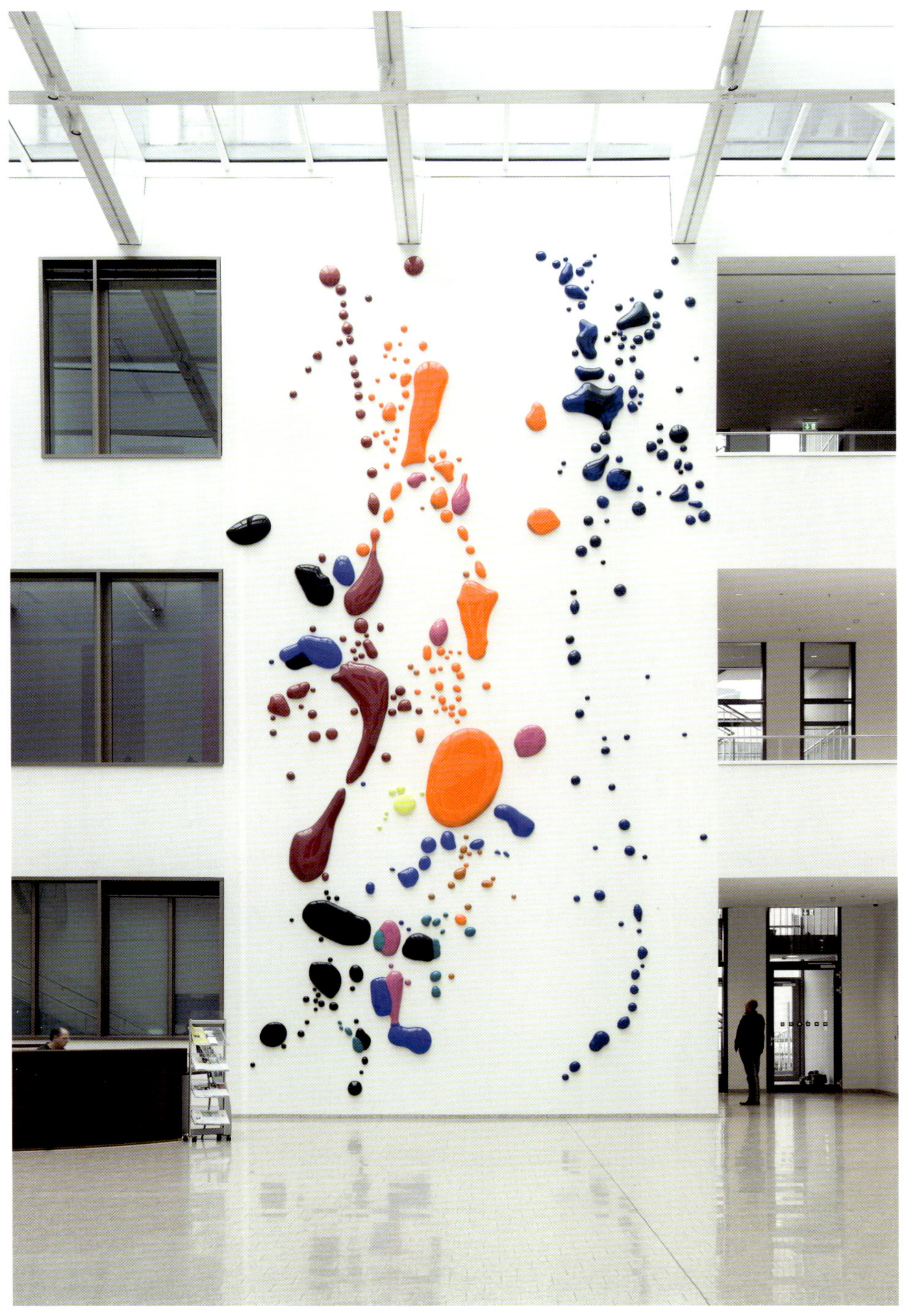

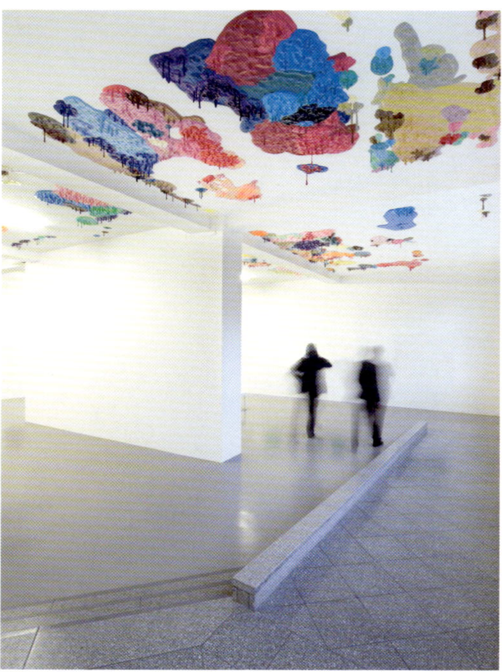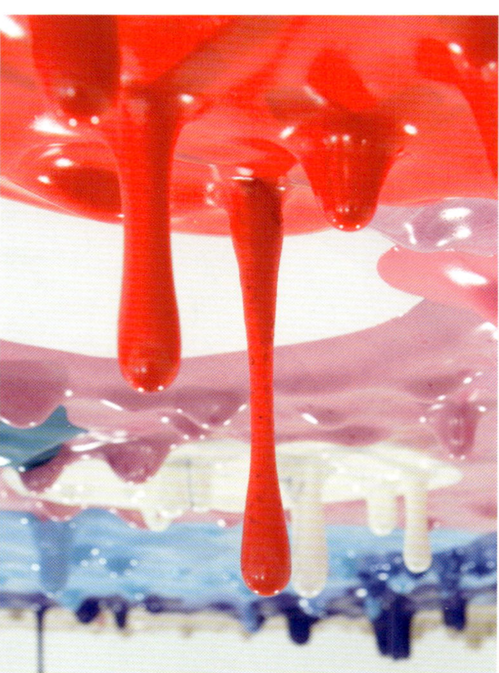

M.F.   Could one speak about a sort of painting that is not binding?

P.Z.   No, the stakes are too high for that. By now, there is simply too much of my life in it. It is true that it is associated with certain physical exertion and wear. It is real effort. In that respect, I think that for me, personally, it is very obligatory, but the question as to whether it has a larger context, with regard to art history or contemporaneity, is a different kettle of fish.

M.F.   Does art open the world of communication?

P.Z.   As an artist, you are always in a dialog situation. You may do your work in a studio, but in the moment you exhibit it, you are in a dialog with your audience.

M.F.   Are you of the opinion, as Gerhard Richter wrote in his early notes, that "now there are no priests or philosophers left, artists are the most important people in the world." (cf. gerhard-richter.com/quotes/kunst-1, Notes 1964-65). Would you attribute this importance to artists?

P.Z.   I would be more reserved. Why are scientists, doctors, or teachers less important for our society? You can take the question even farther: Why is a homeless person insignificant? Maybe it is also simply true that creativity is not limited to certain professions.

M.F.   There are many jobs that are significant for people to live together.

P.Z.   In an ant colony, there are not only queens, but also workers and drones. There, differentiation is the ultimate guarantor of survival.

"M.A.P" 2006
Epoxy resin on aluminum panel
700 x 500 cm / 29.6 x 91 feet

M.A.P 2006年
環氧樹脂于鋁板上
700 x 500公分 / 29.6 x 91英呎

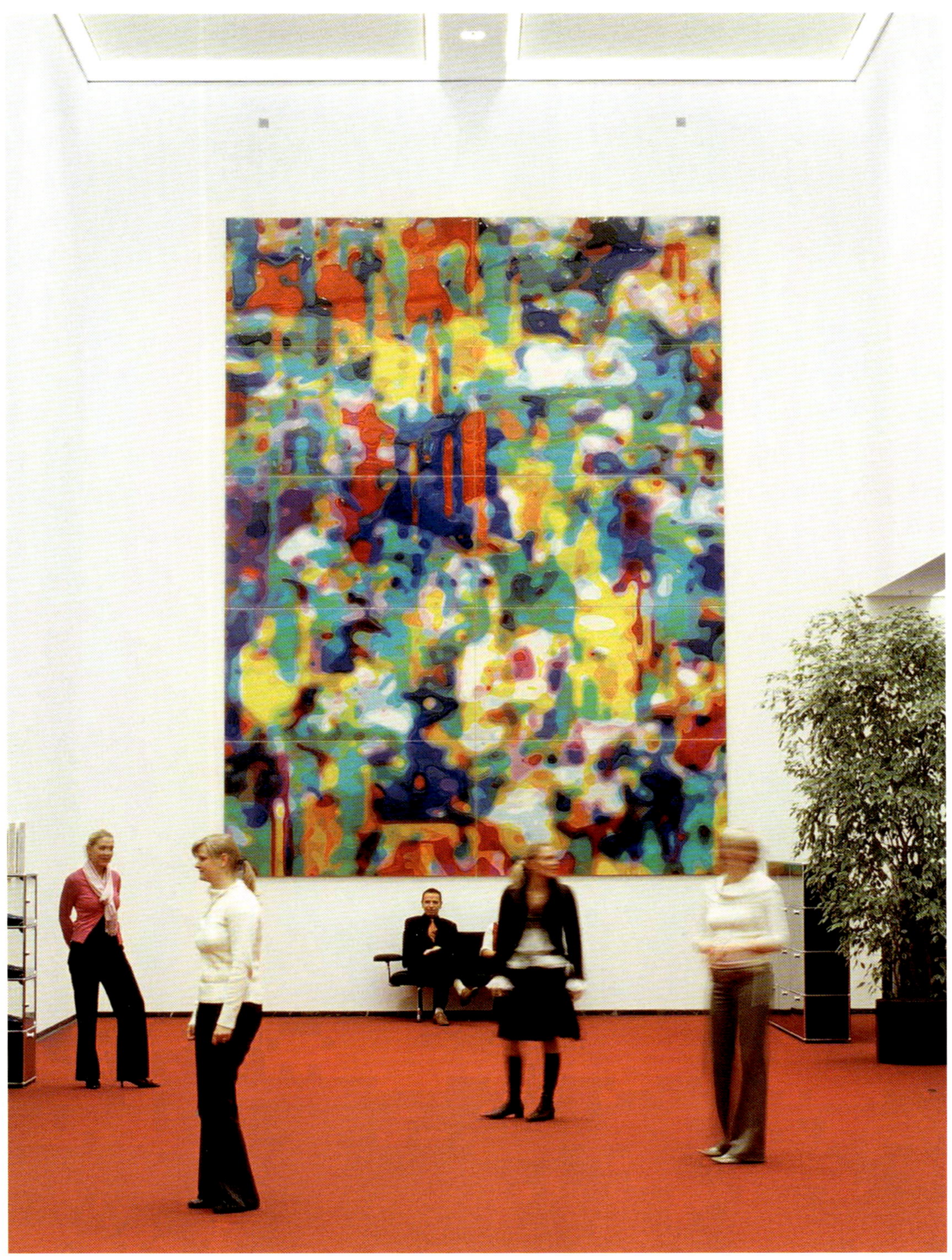

Kith and Kin

親友

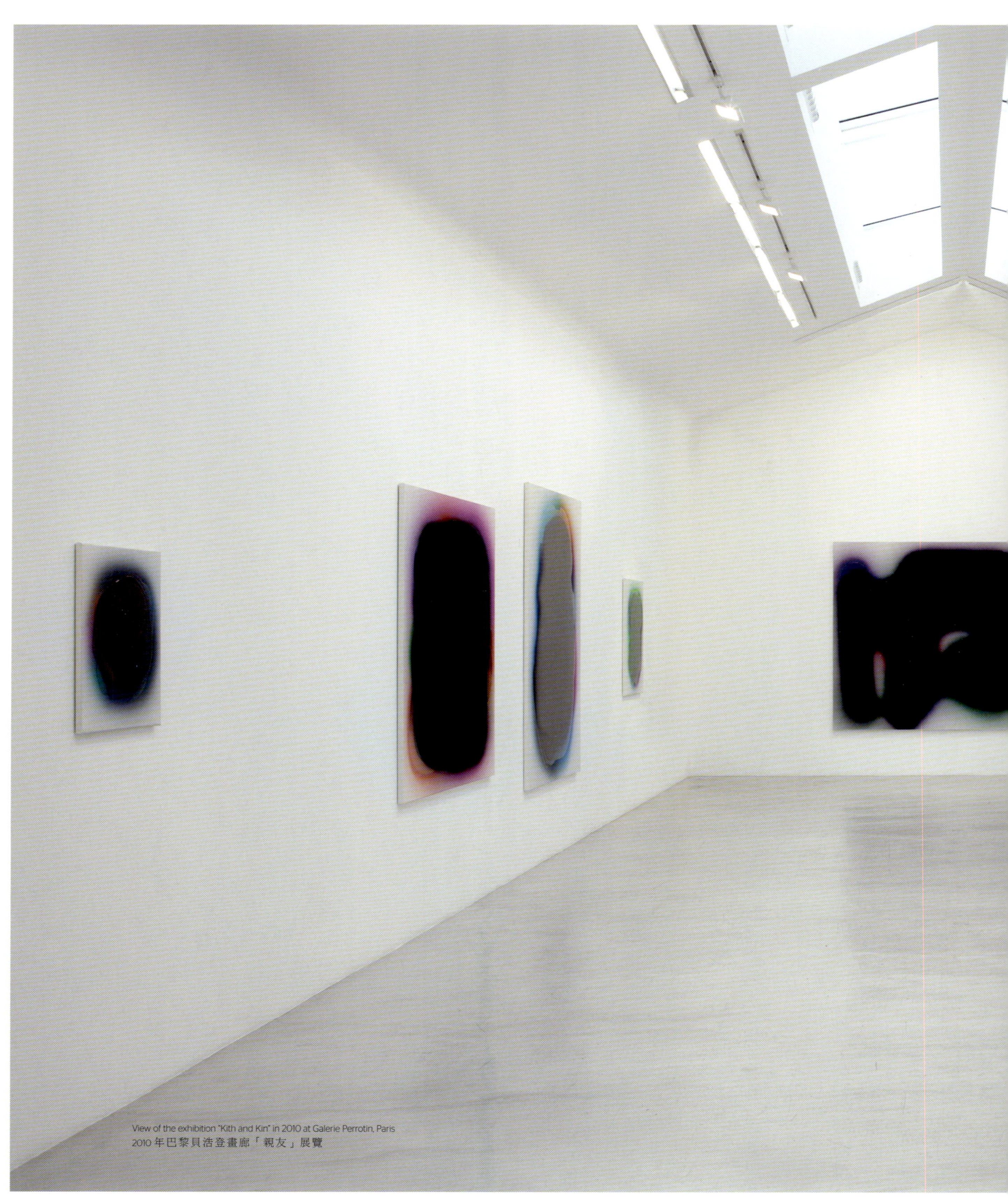

View of the exhibition "Kith and Kin" in 2010 at Galerie Perrotin, Paris
2010 年巴黎貝浩登畫廊「親友」展覽

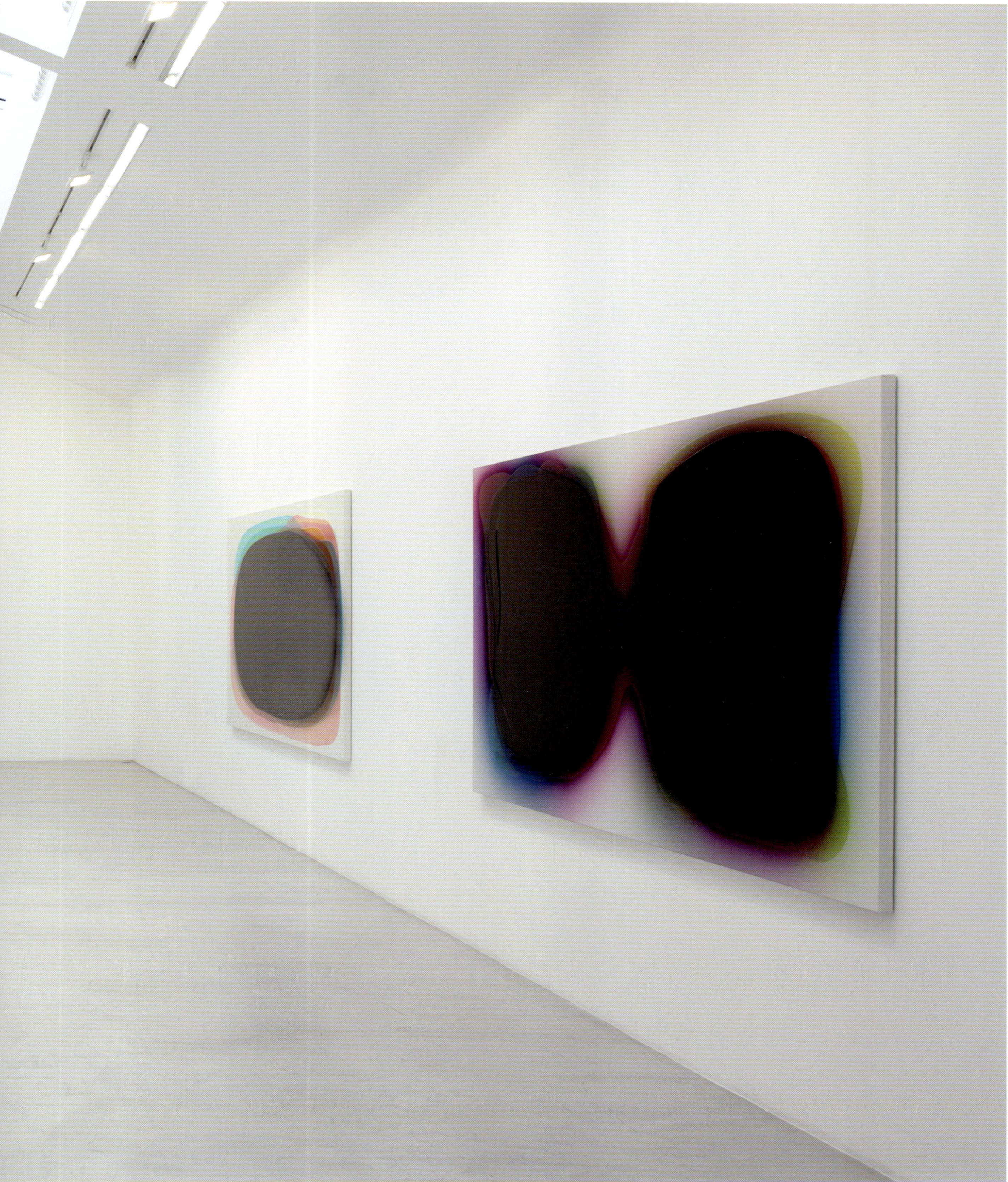

"Saturn P." 2010
Acrylic and epoxy resin on canvas
100 x 80 cm / 39 1/2 x 31 inches

薩圖恩.P. 2010 年
　與環氧樹脂帆布畫
100 x 80公分 / 39 1/2 x 31英吋

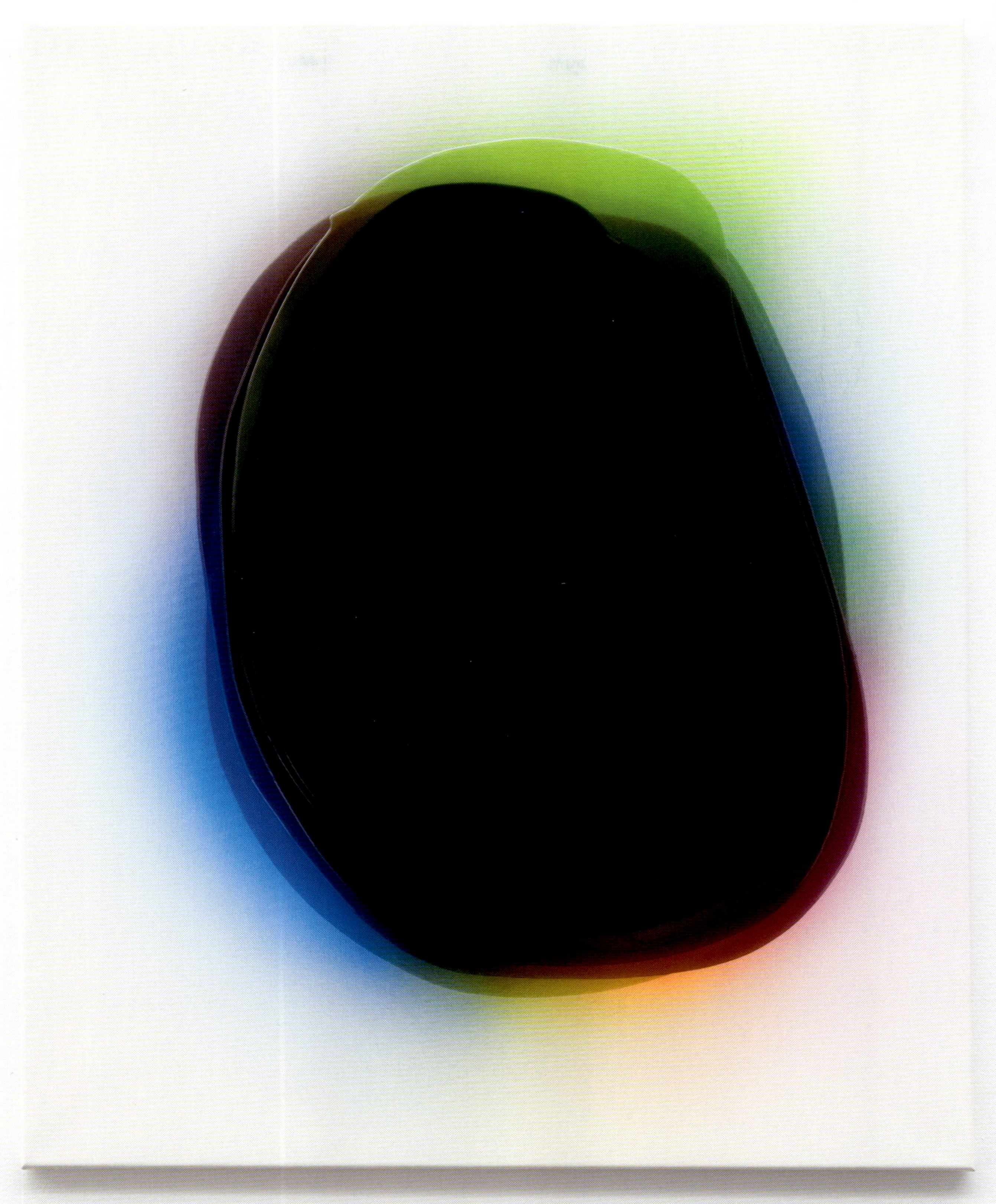

"Cyrus Z." 2010
Acrylic and epoxy resin on canvas
120 x 100 cm / 47 1/4 x 39 1/2 inches

居魯士Z. 2010年
丙烯與環氧樹脂帆布畫
120 x 100公分 / 47 1/4 x 39 1/2英吋

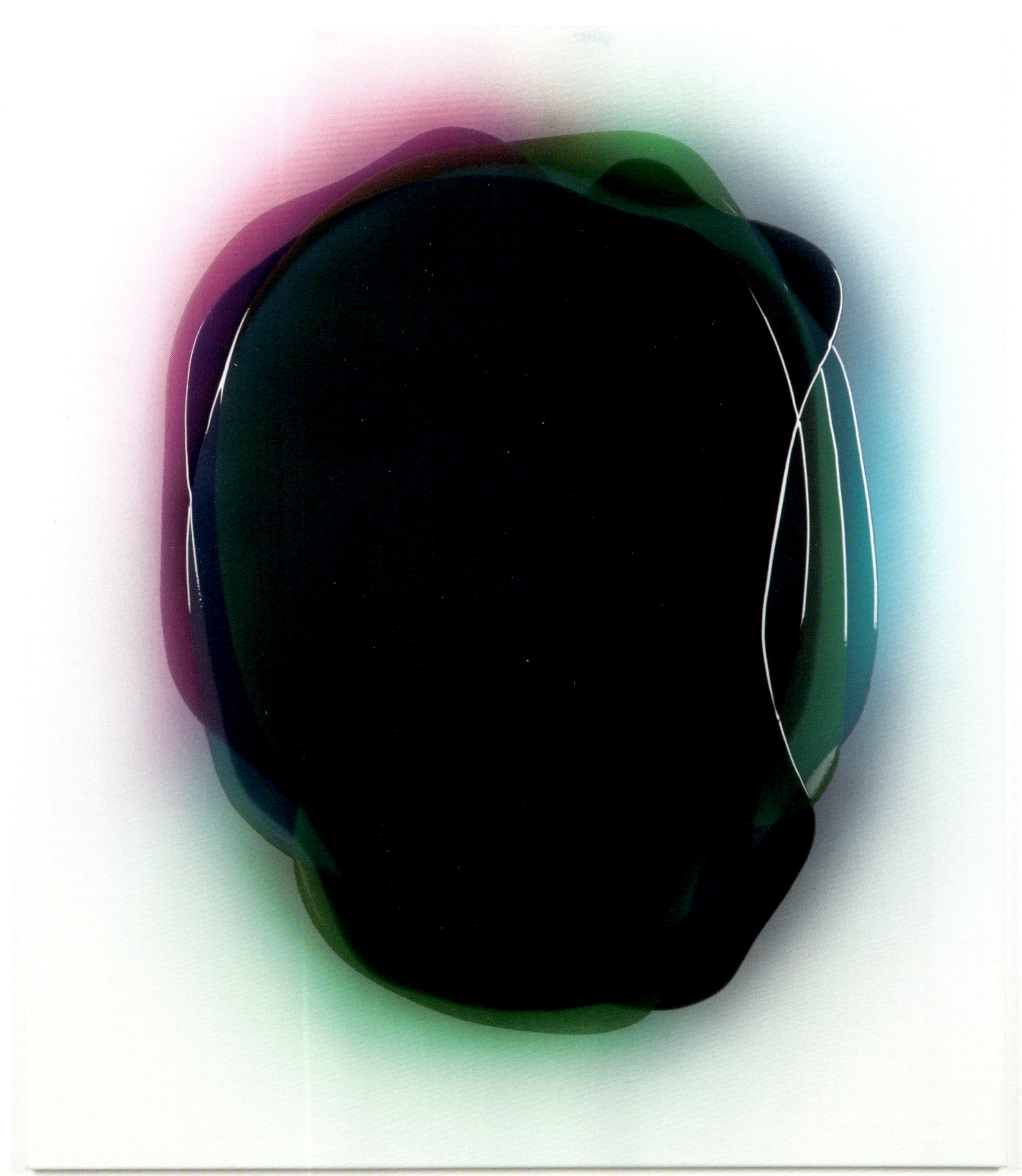

"Lance K." 2010
Acrylic and epoxy resin on canvas
180 x 130 cm / 70.9 x 51 inches

蘭斯 K. 2010 年
丙烯與環氧樹脂帆布畫
180 x 130公分 / 70.9 x 51英吋

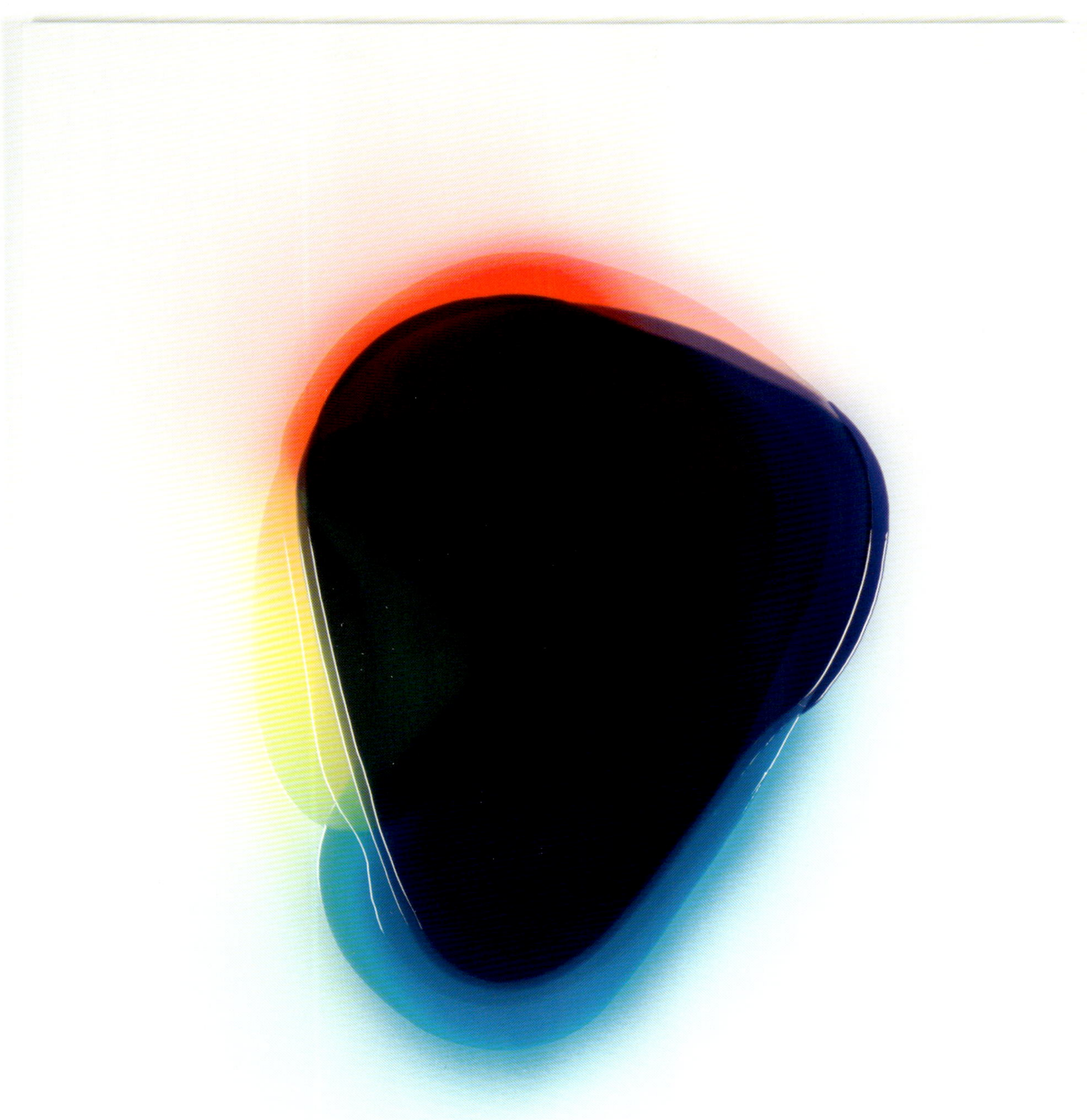

"Neela N." 2010
Acrylic and epoxy resin on canvas
200 x 145 cm / 6.6 feet x 57 inches

妮拉 N. 2010年
丙烯與環氧樹脂帆布畫
200 x 145公分 / 6.6英呎 x 57英吋

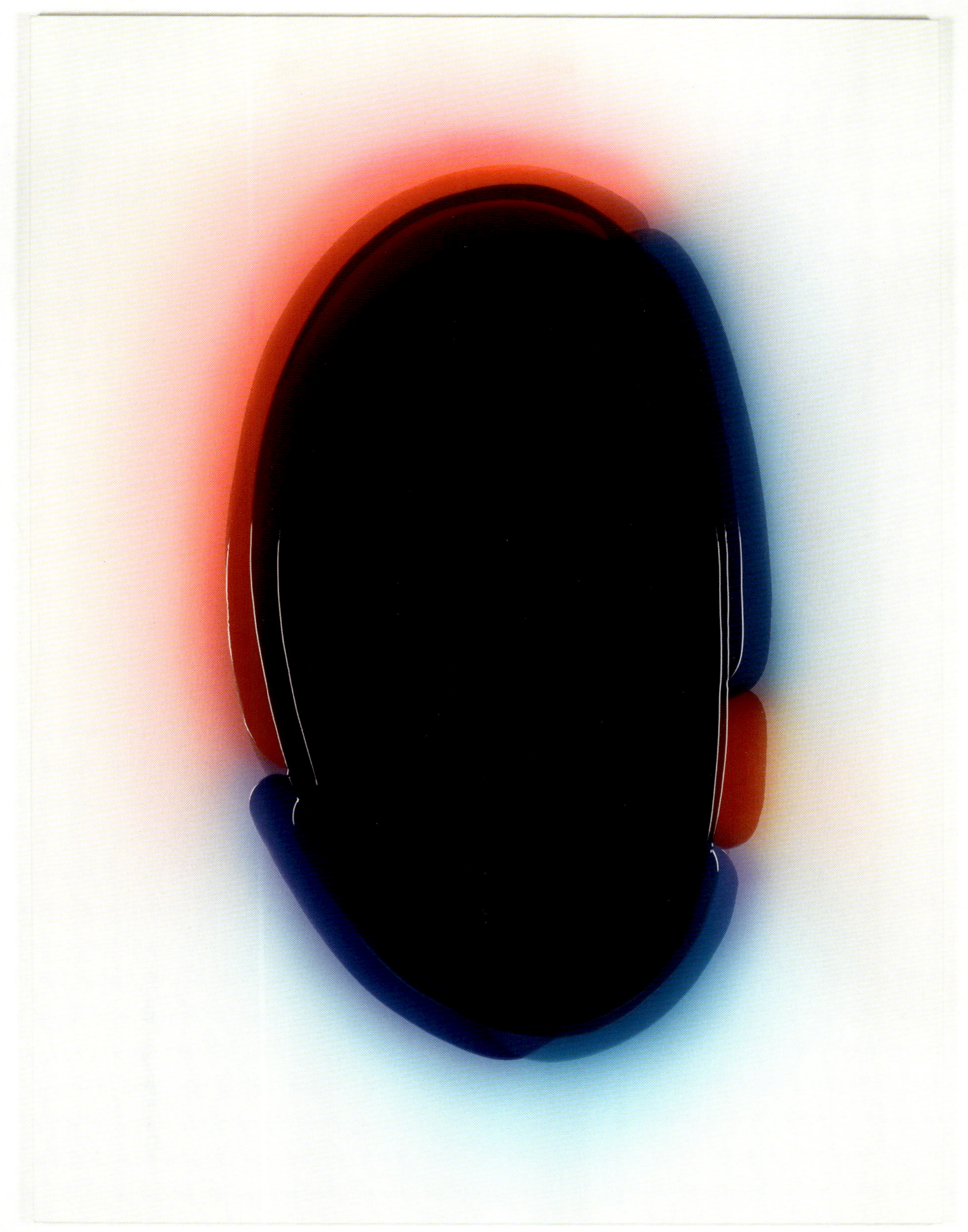

"Sandysea P." 2010
Acrylic and epoxy resin on canvas
200 x 145 cm / 6.6 feet x 57 inches

珊蒂斯 P. 2010年
丙烯與環氧樹脂帆布畫
200 x 145公分 / 6.6英呎 x 57英吋

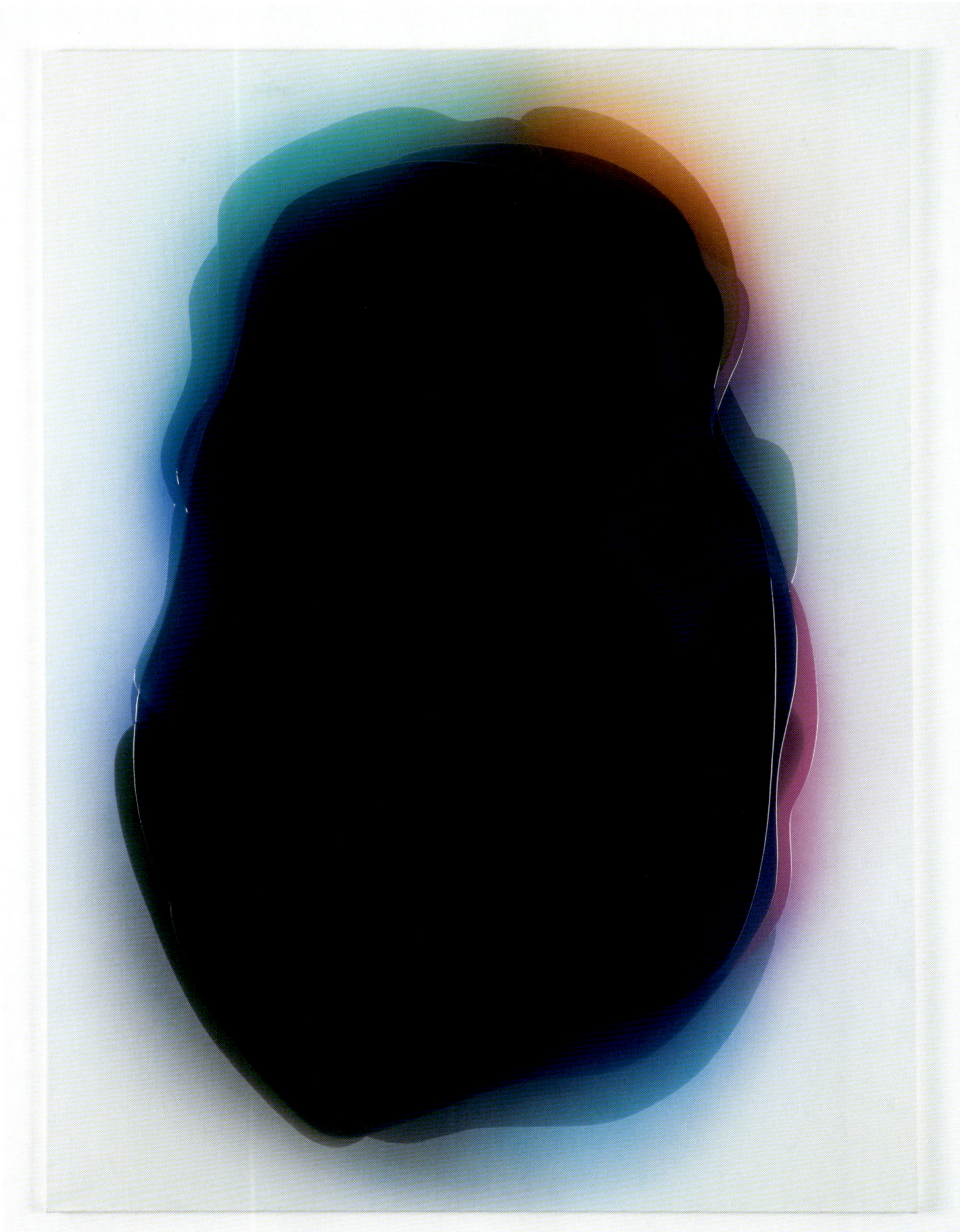

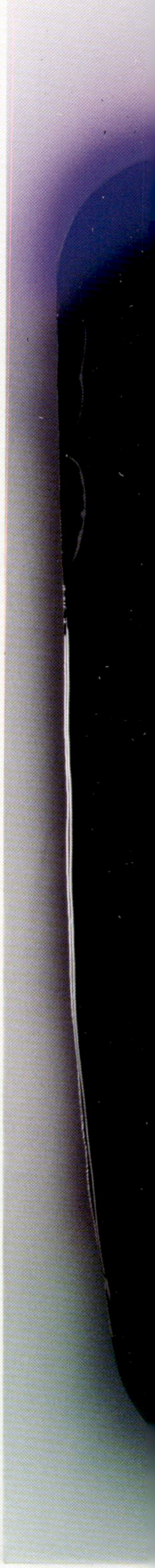

"M.S.H." 2010
Acrylic and epoxy resin on canvas
200 x 200 cm / 6.6 x 6.6 feet

M.S.H. 2010年
丙烯與環氧樹脂帆布畫
200 x 200 公分 / 6.6 x 6.6 英呎

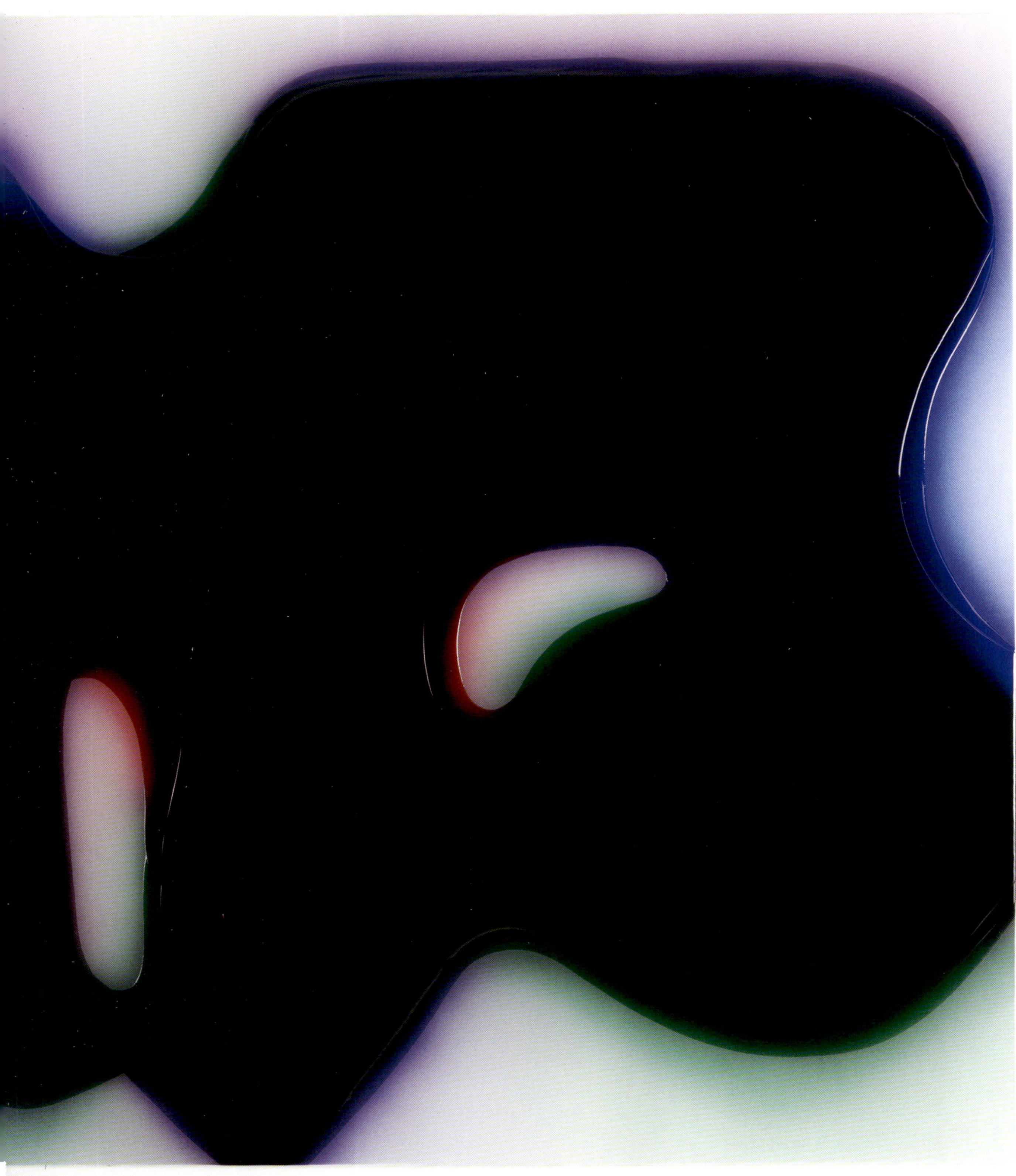

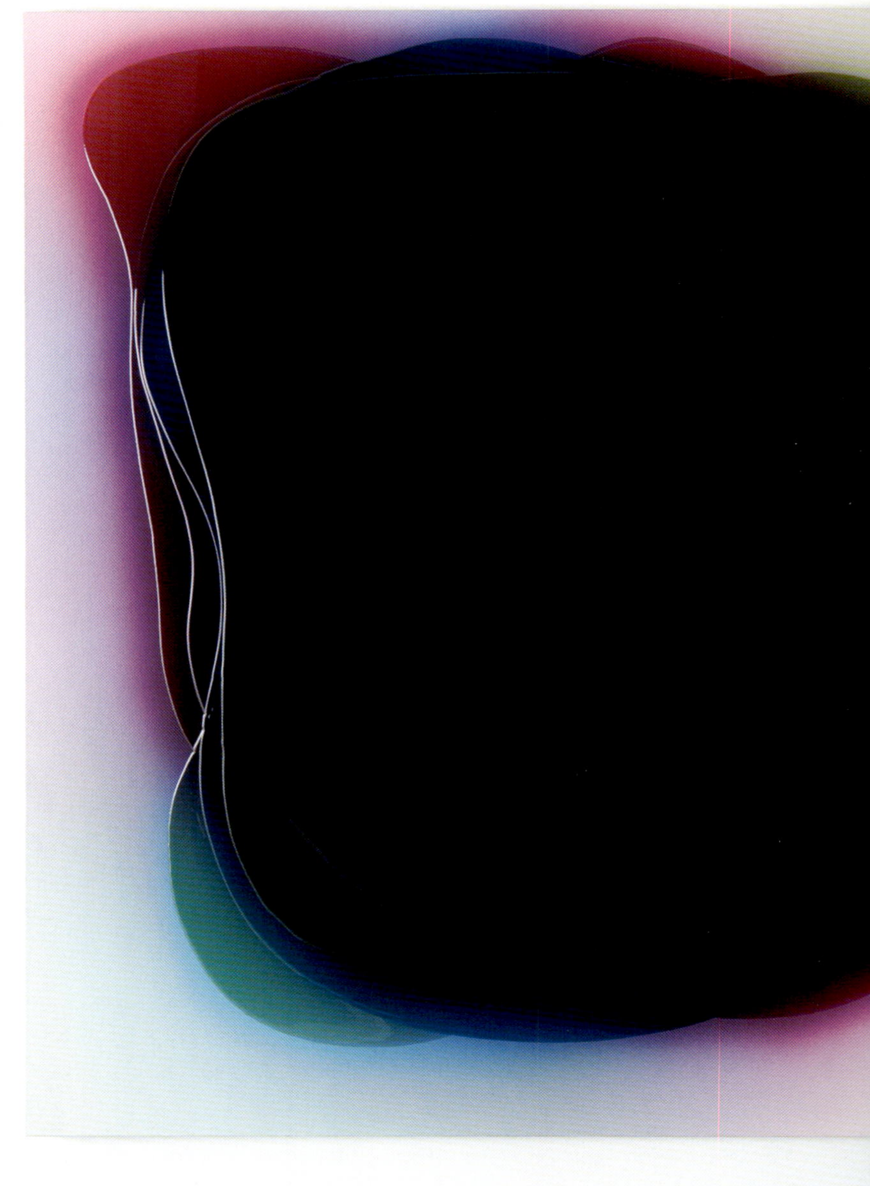

"Kiss" 2010
Acrylic and Epoxy resin on canvas
150 x 300 cm / 59 inches x 9.1 feet

吻 2010年
丙烯與環氧樹脂帆布畫
150 x 300公分 ／ 59 x 9.1英呎

46

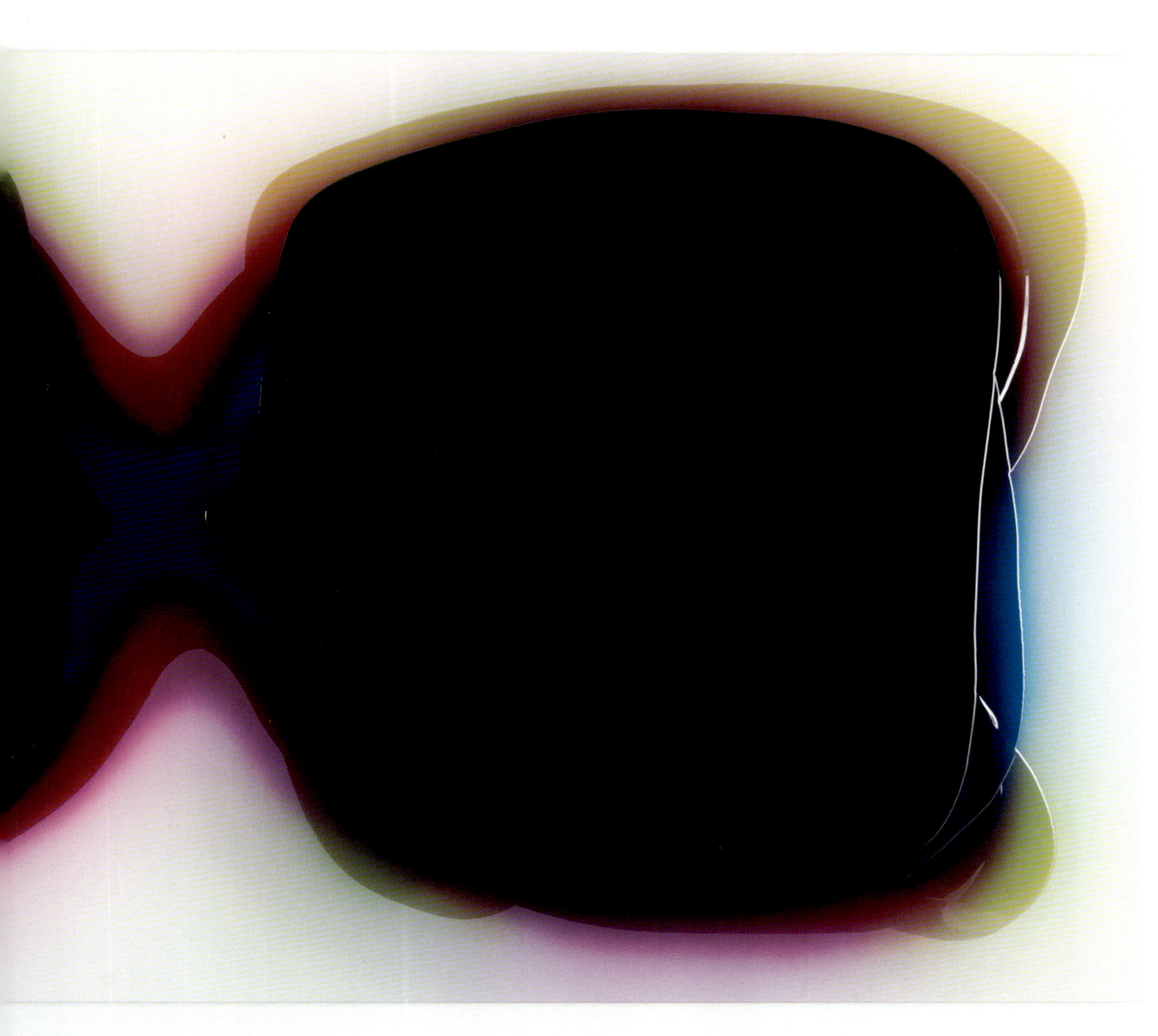

D.E.E.P.

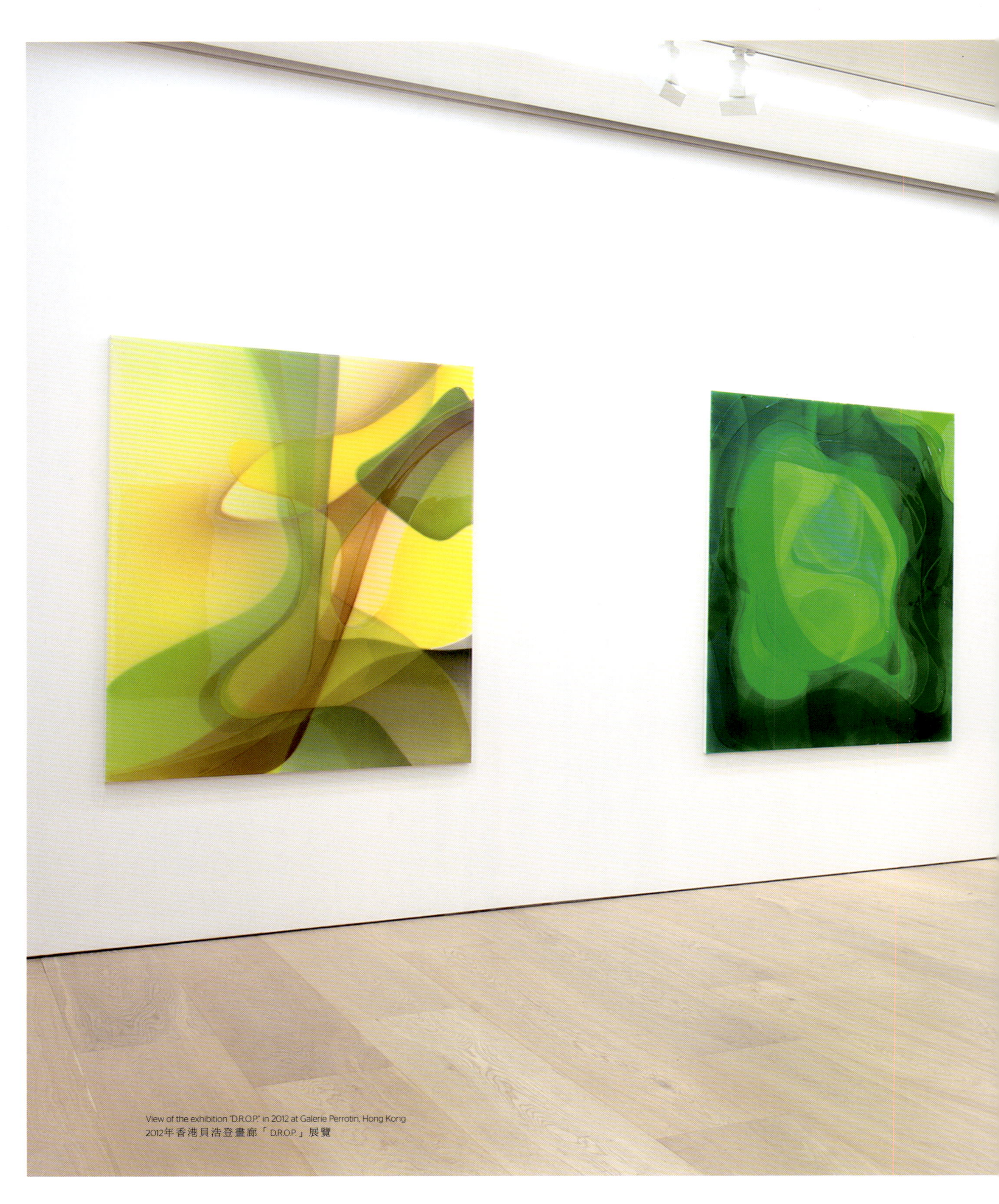

View of the exhibition "D.R.O.P." in 2012 at Galerie Perrotin, Hong Kong
2012年香港貝浩登畫廊「D.R.O.P.」展覽

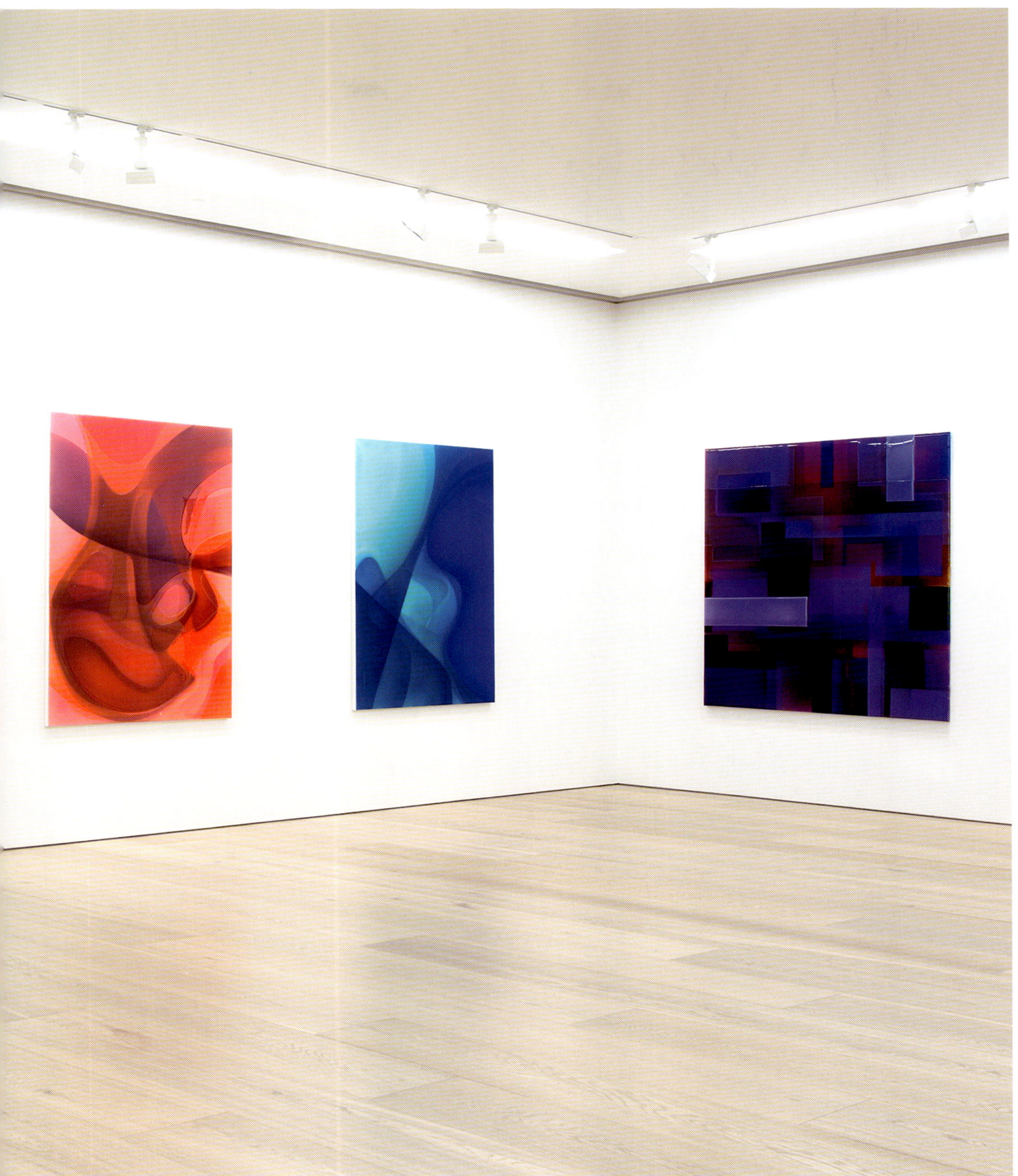

"D.E.E.P. 2" 2012
Epoxy resin on canvas
150 x 110 cm / 59 x 47 1/4 inches

D.E.E.P.2 2012年
環氧樹脂帆布畫
150 x 110公分 / 59 x 47 1/4英吋

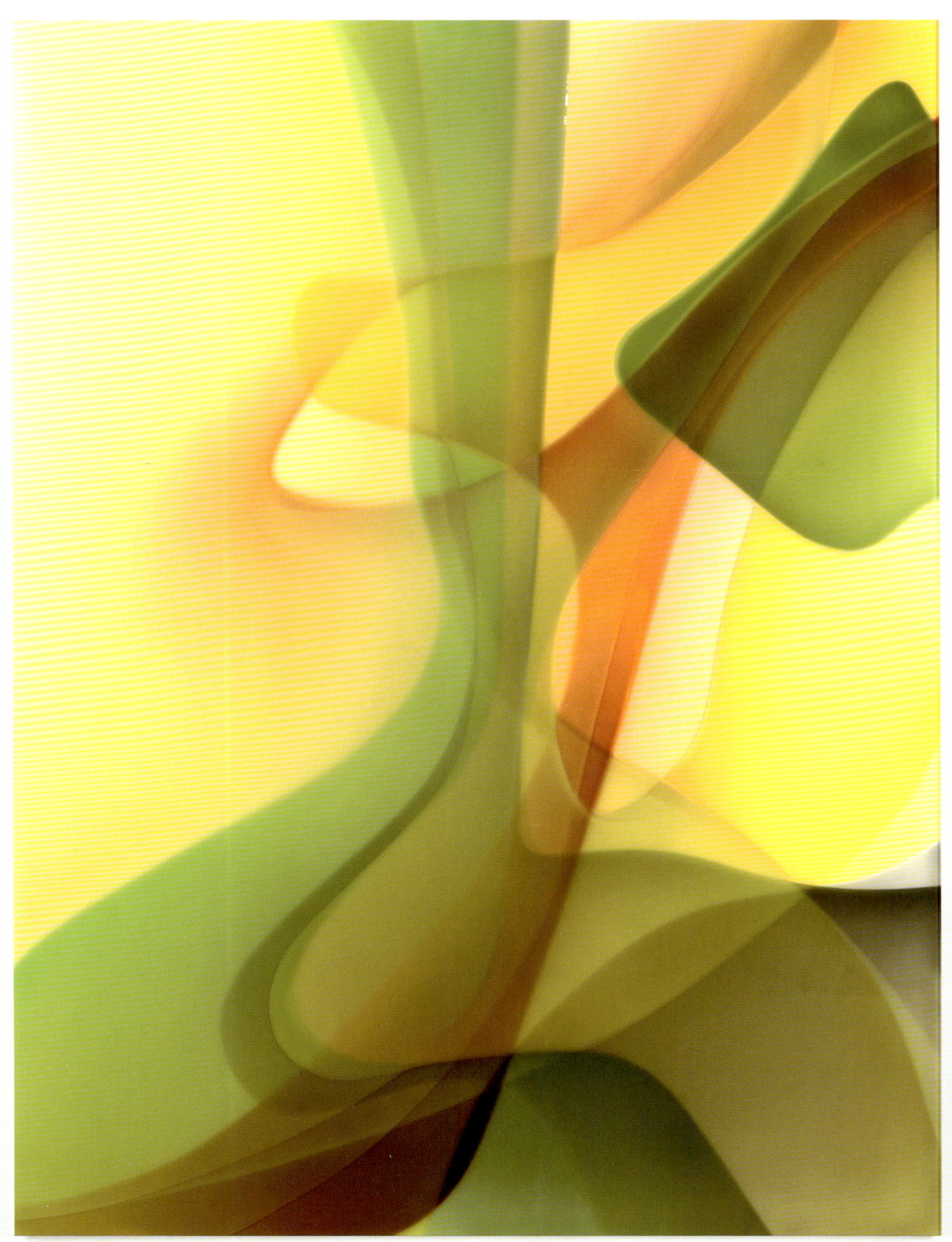

"D.E.E.P. 3" 2012
Epoxy resin on canvas
150 x 110 cm / 59 x 43 1/4 inches

D.E.E.P.3 2012年
環氧樹脂帆布畫
150 x 110公分 / 59 x 43 1/4英吋

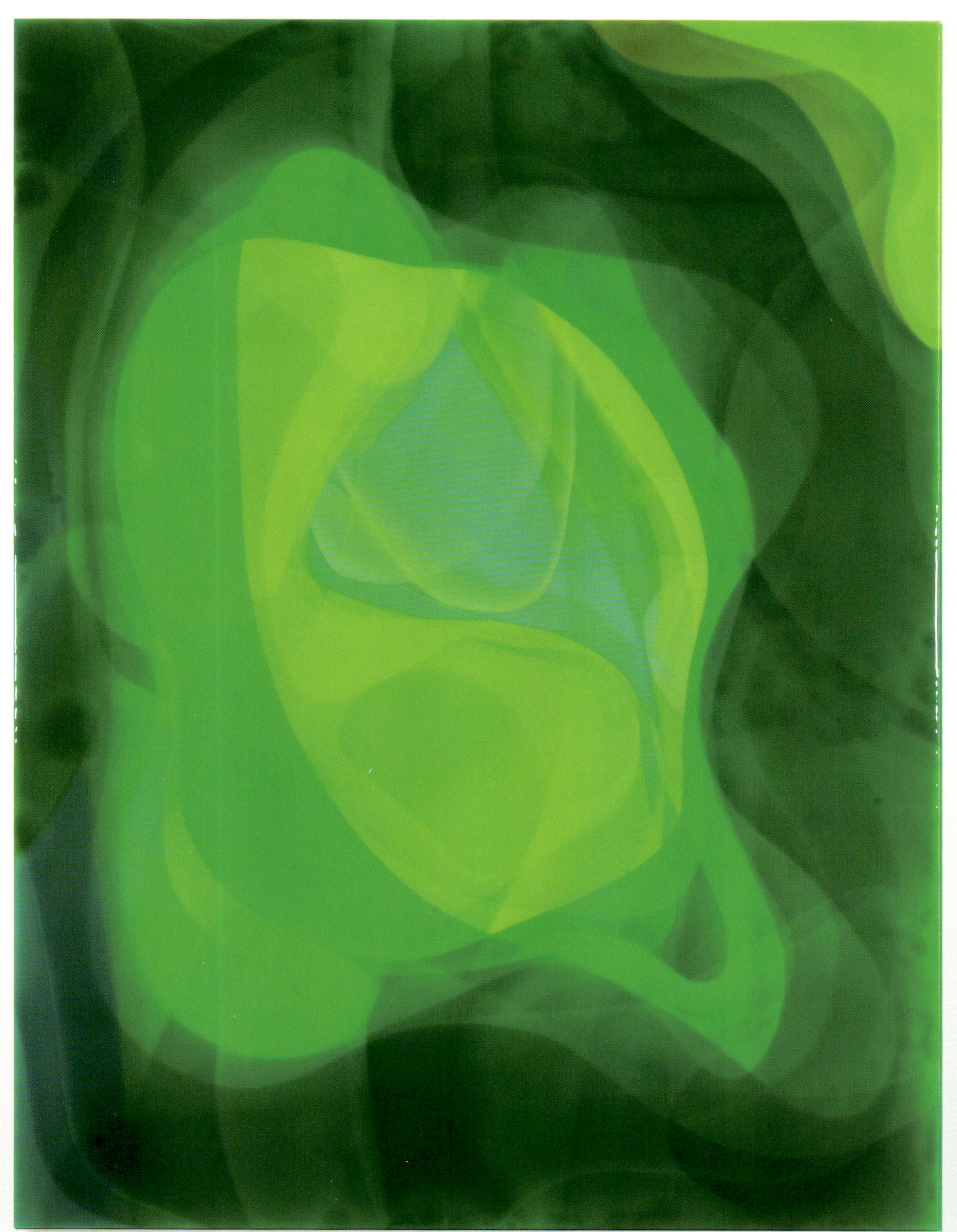

"D.E.E.P. 4" 2012
Epoxy resin on canvas
150 x 110 cm / 59 x 43 1/4 inches

D.E.E.P.4 2012年
環氧樹脂帆布畫
150 x 110公分 / 59 x 43 1/4英吋

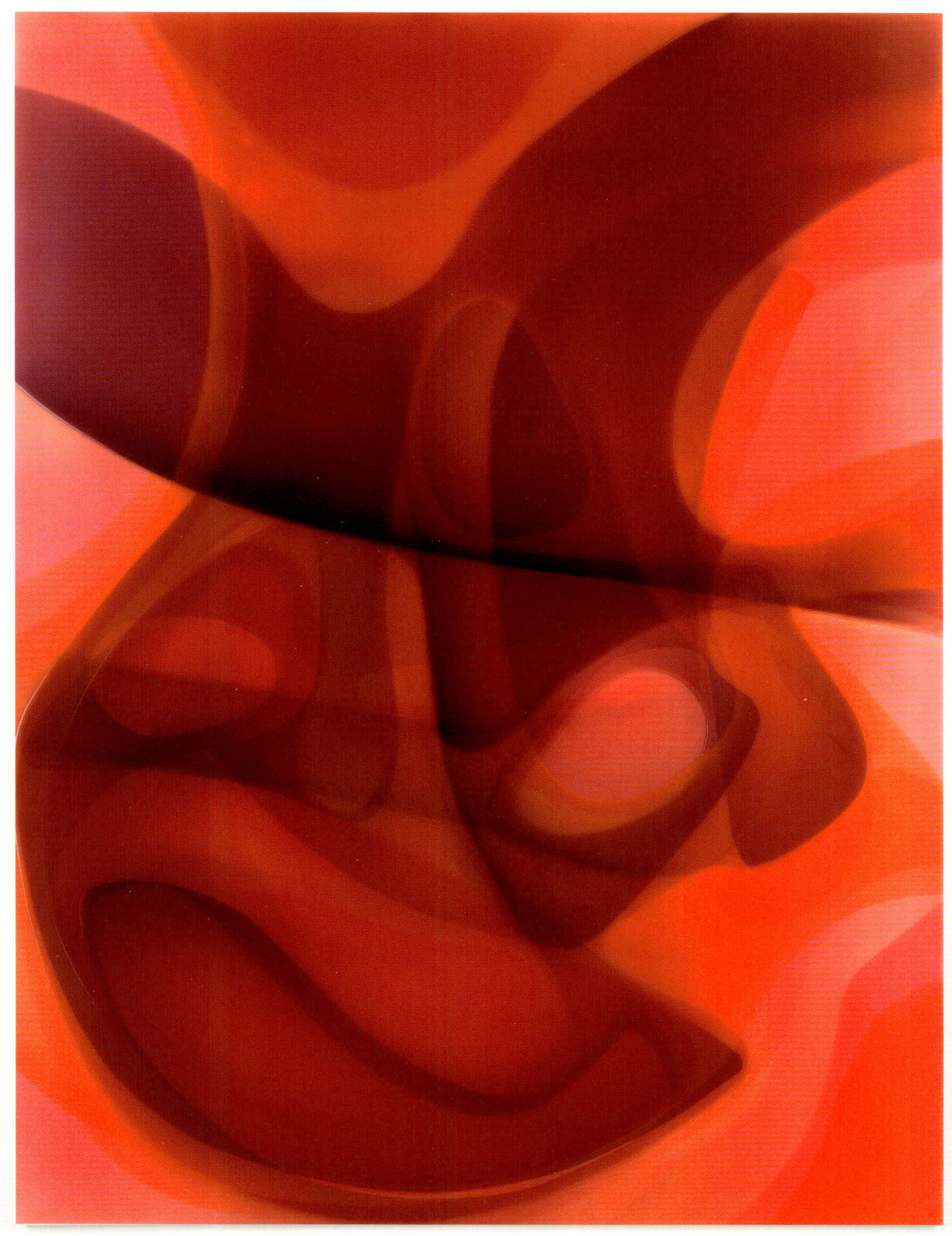

"D.E.E.P. 5" 2012
Epoxy resin on canvas
150 x 110 cm / 59 x 43 1/4 inches

D.E.E.P.5 2012年
環氧樹脂帆布畫
150 x 110 公分 / 59 x 43 1/4 英吋

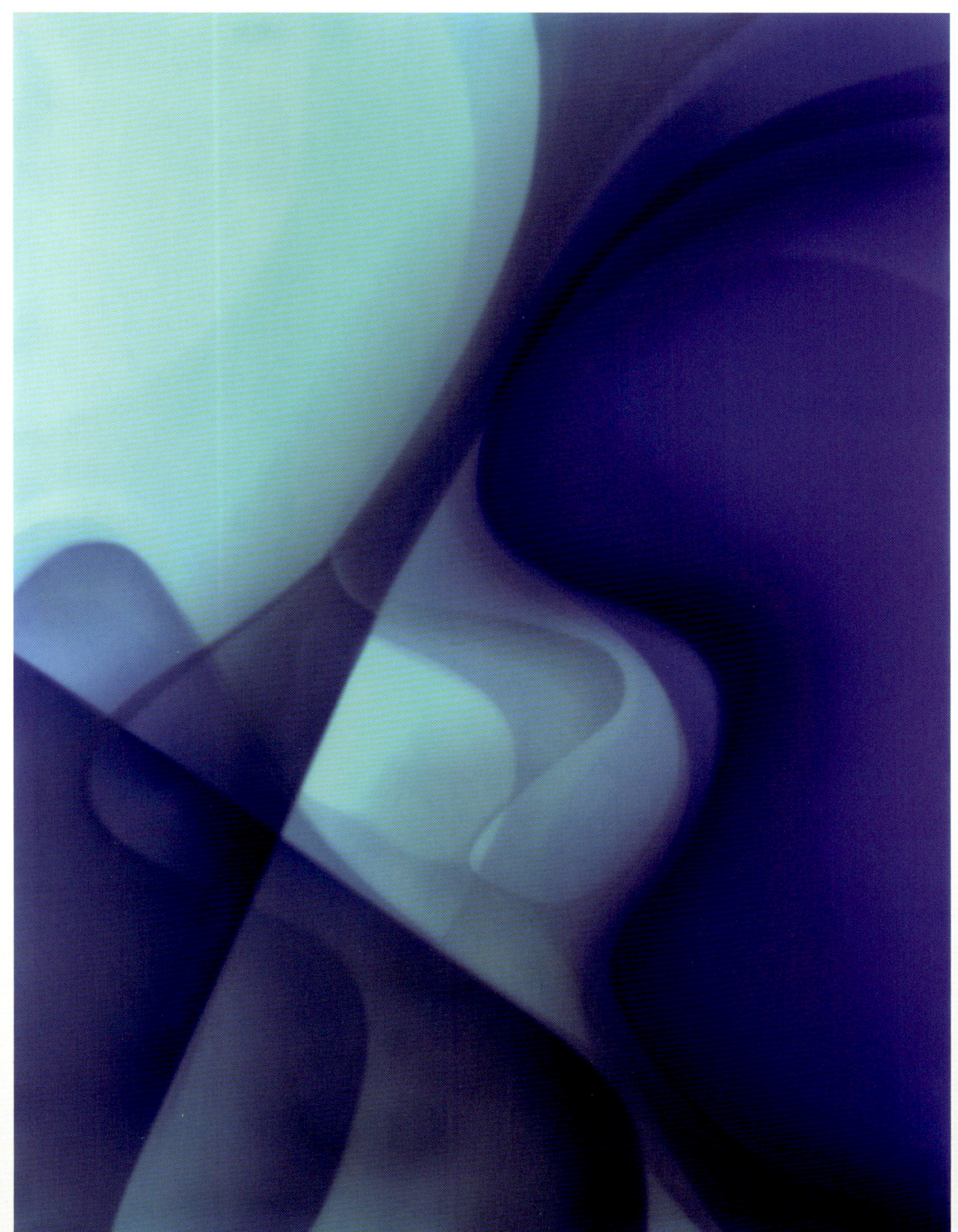

"bass" 2012
Epoxy resin on canvas
150 x 120 cm / 59 x 47 1/4 inches

低音吉他 2012年
環氧樹脂帆布畫
150 x 120 公分 / 59 x 47 1/4 英吋

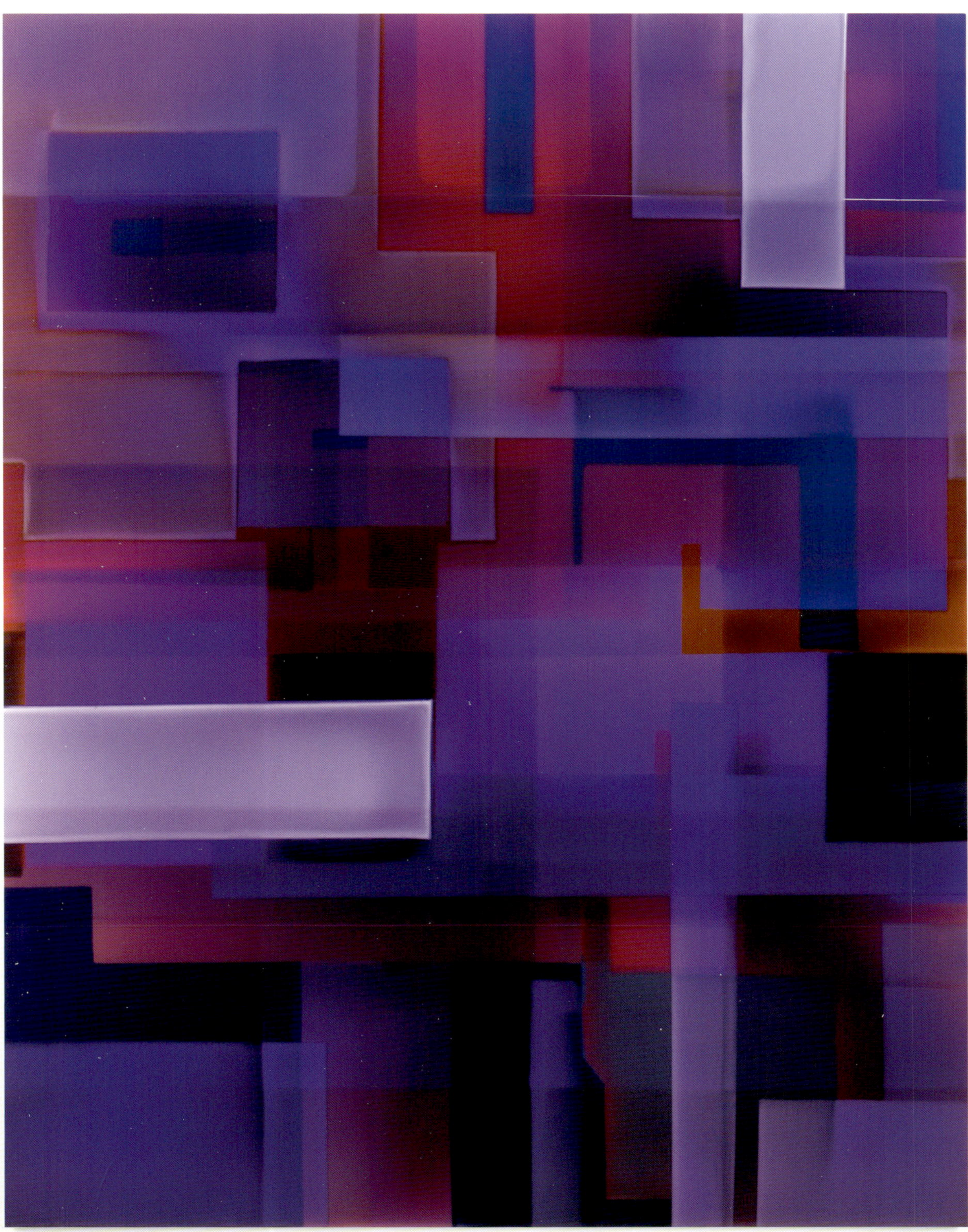

STROKE

划

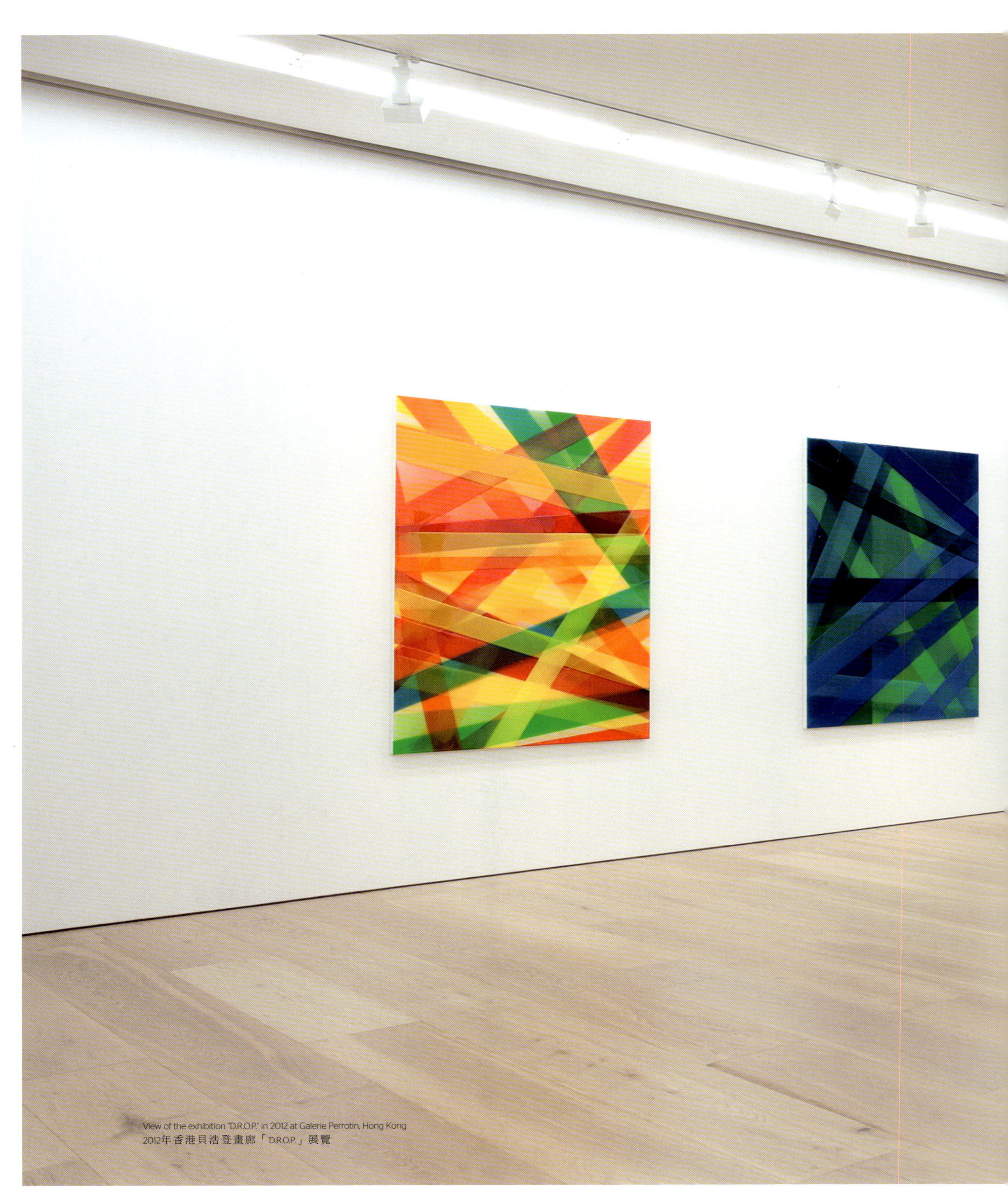
View of the exhibition "D.R.O.P." in 2012 at Galerie Perrotin, Hong Kong
2012年香港貝浩登畫廊「D.R.O.P.」展覽

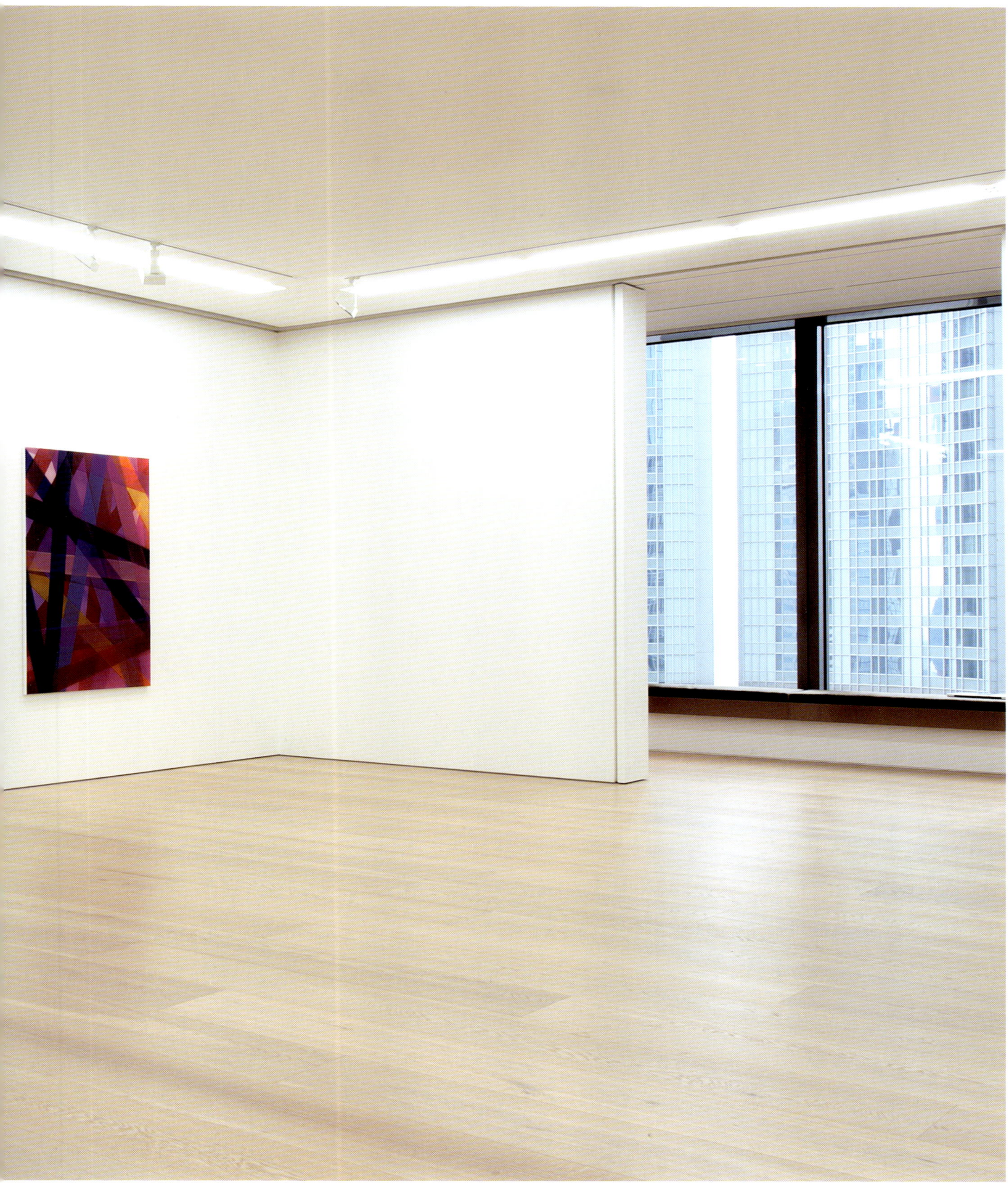

"stroke I" 2012
Epoxy resin on canvas
150 x 110 cm / 59 x 43 1/4 inches

划I   2012 年
環氧樹脂帆布畫
150 x 110公分 / 59 x 43 1/4英吋

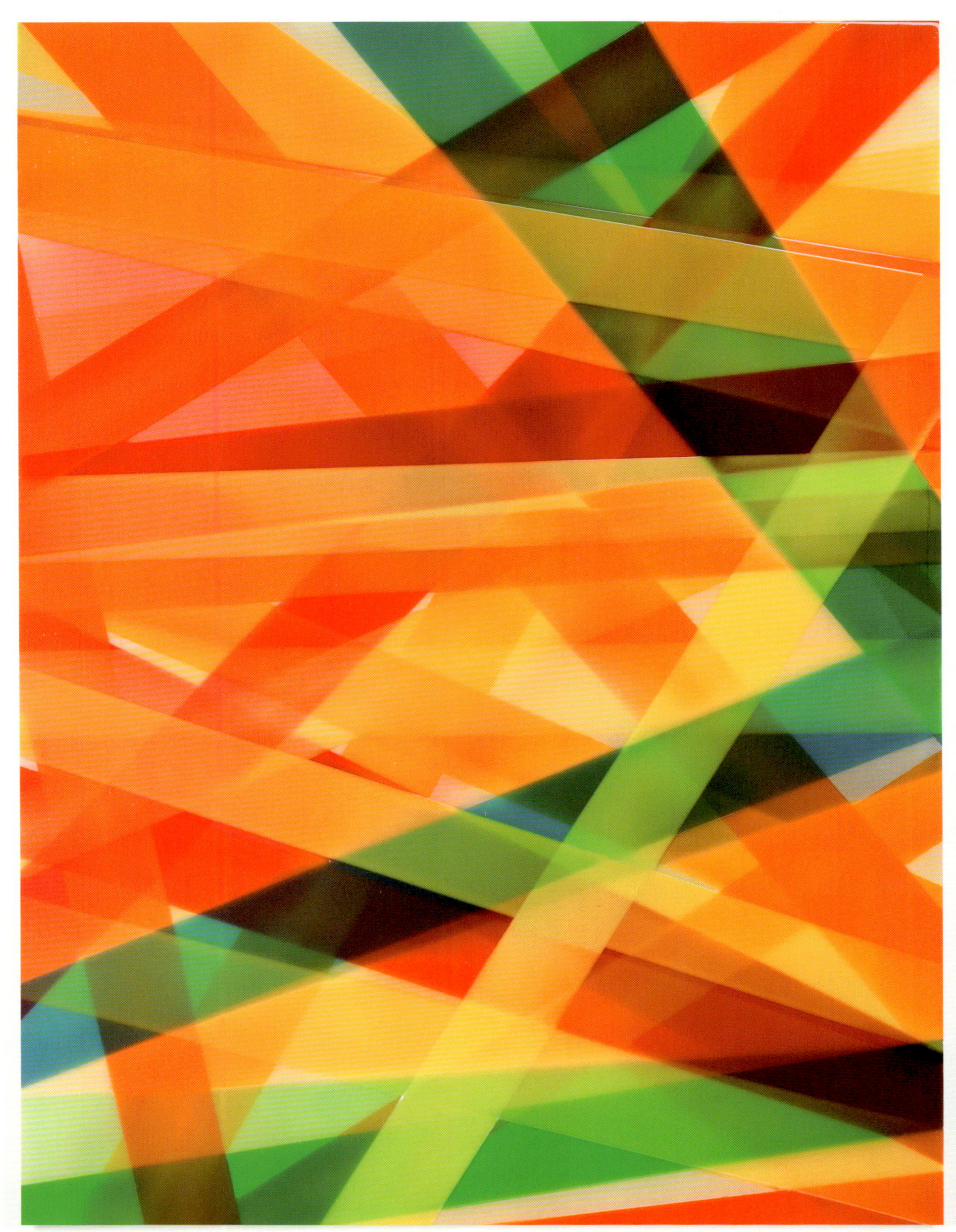

"stroke II" 2012
Epoxy resin on canvas
150 x 110 cm / 59 x 43 1/4 inches

划 II 2012 年
環氧樹脂帆布畫
150 x 110公分 / 59 x 43 1/4英吋

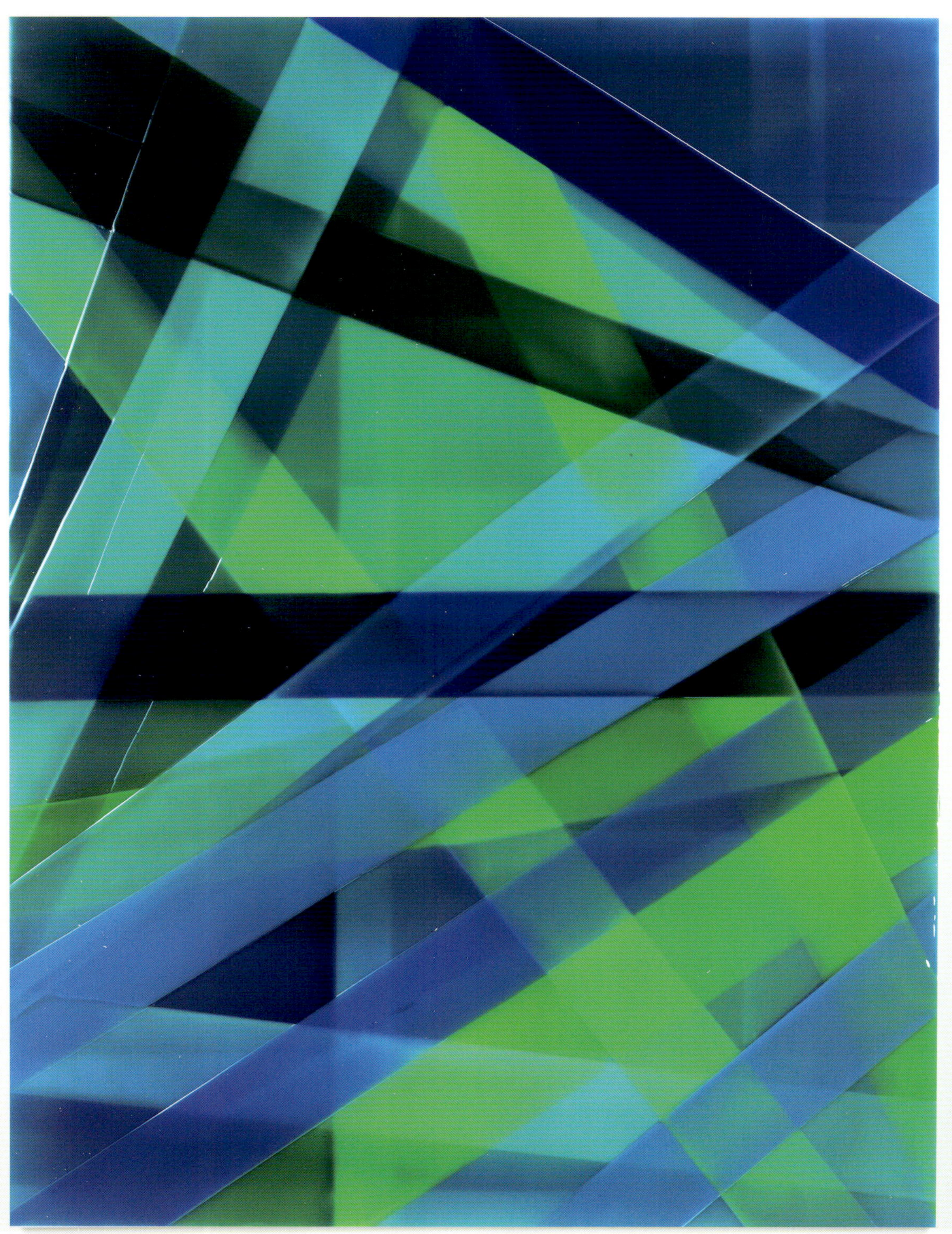

"stroke III" 2012
Epoxy resin on canvas
150 x 110 cm / 59 x 43 1/4 inches

划 III 2012 年
環氧樹脂帆布畫
150 x 110公分 / 59 x 43 1/4英吋

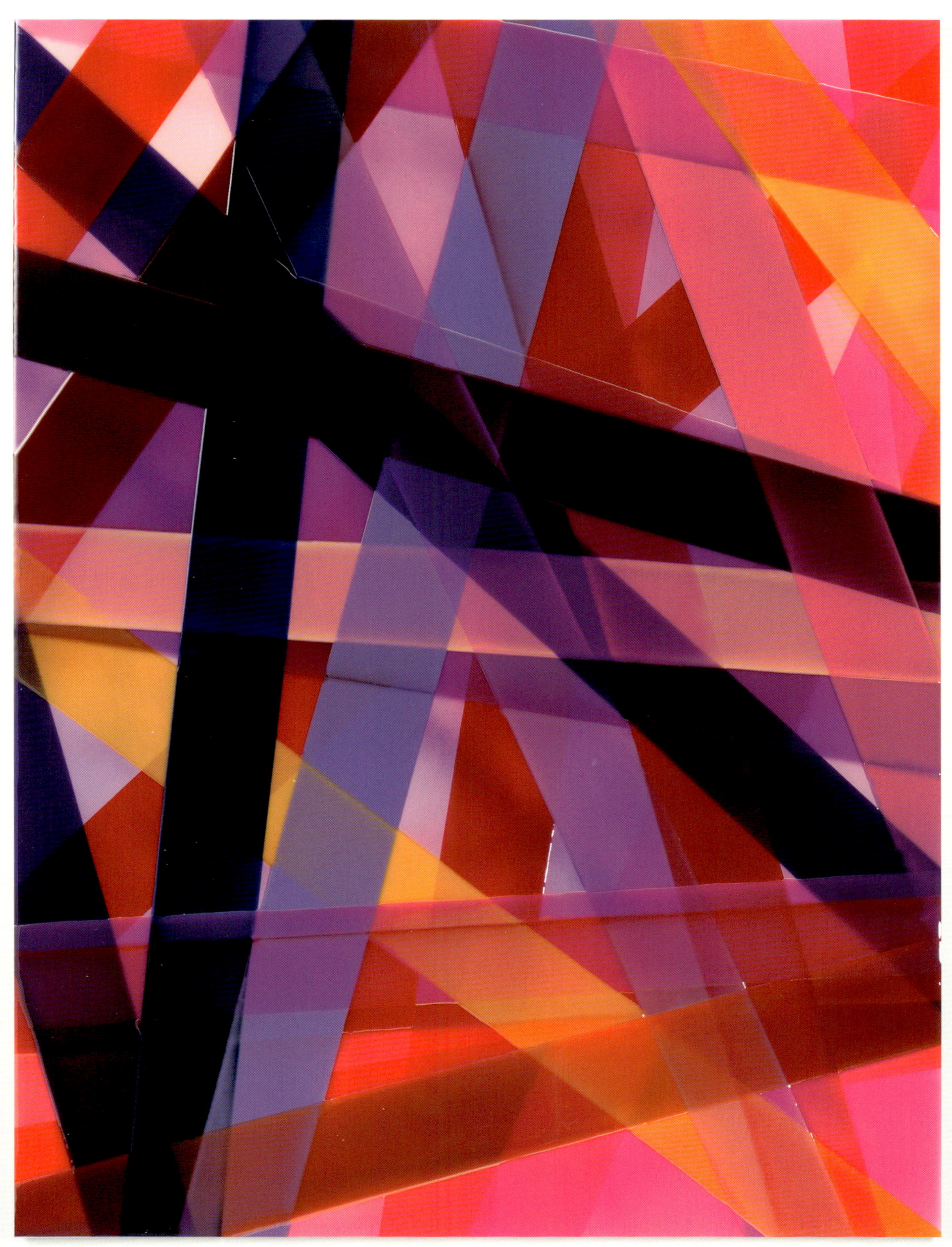

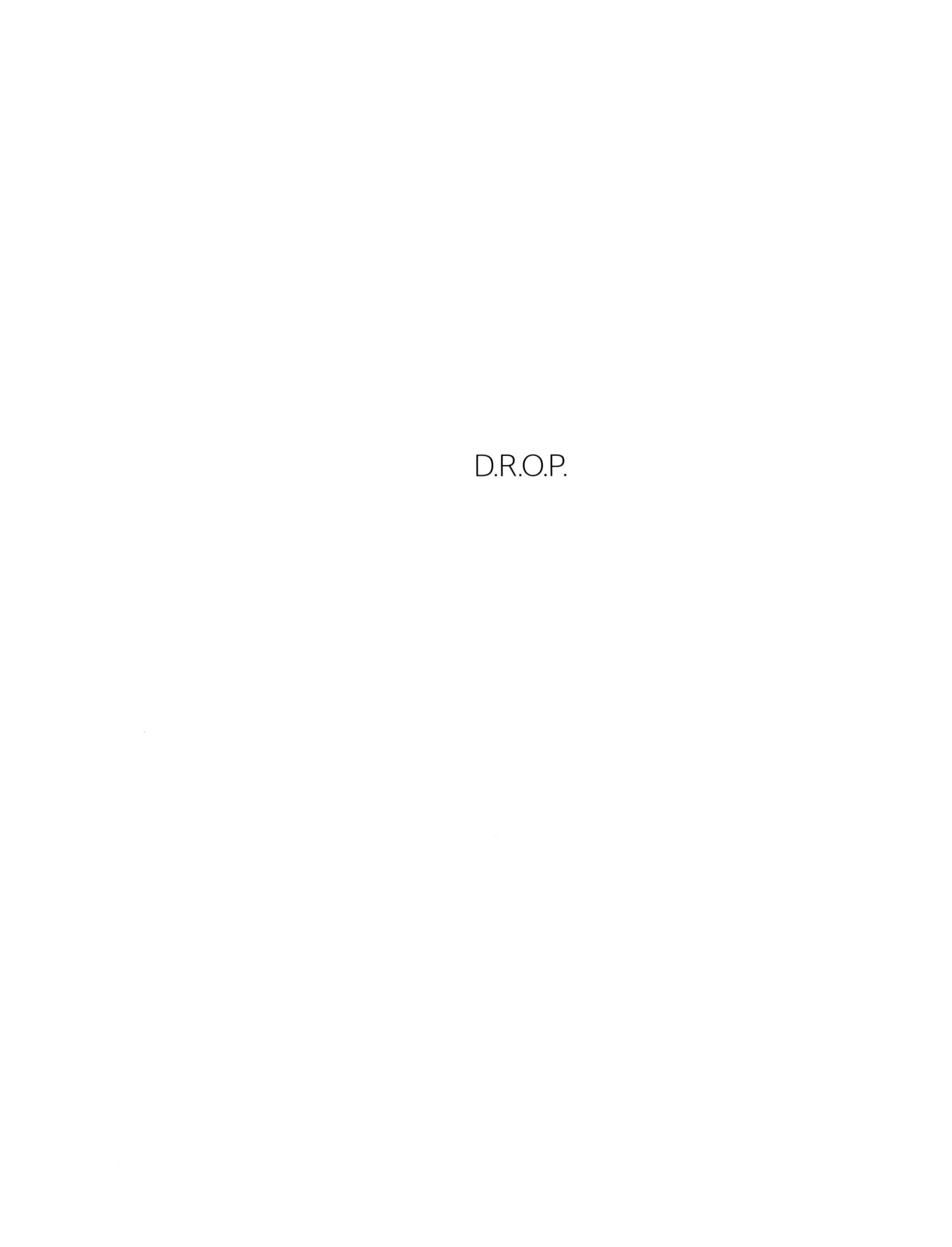

D.R.O.P.

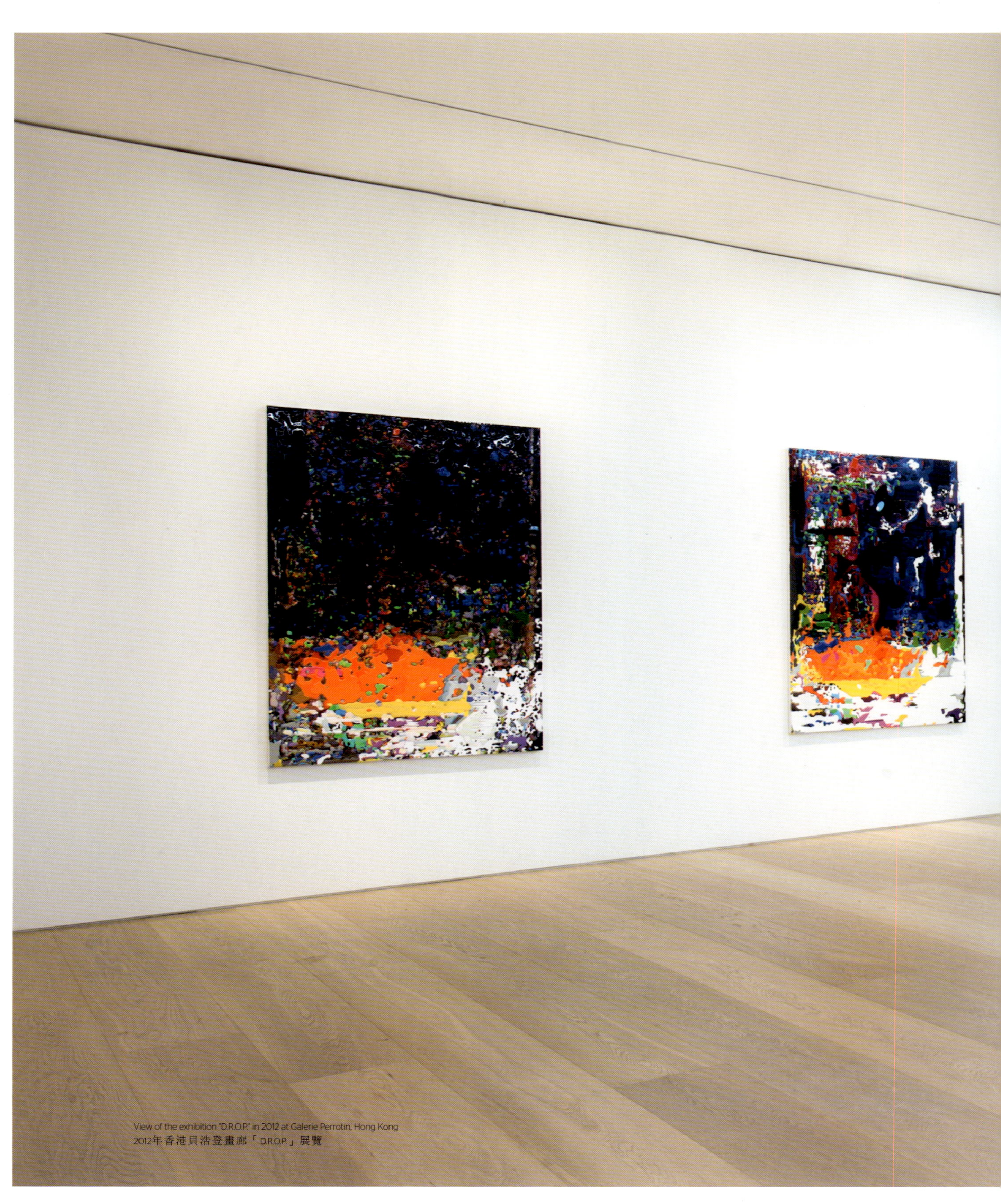

View of the exhibition "D.R.O.P." in 2012 at Galerie Perrotin, Hong Kong
2012年 香港貝浩登畫廊「D.R.O.P.」展覽

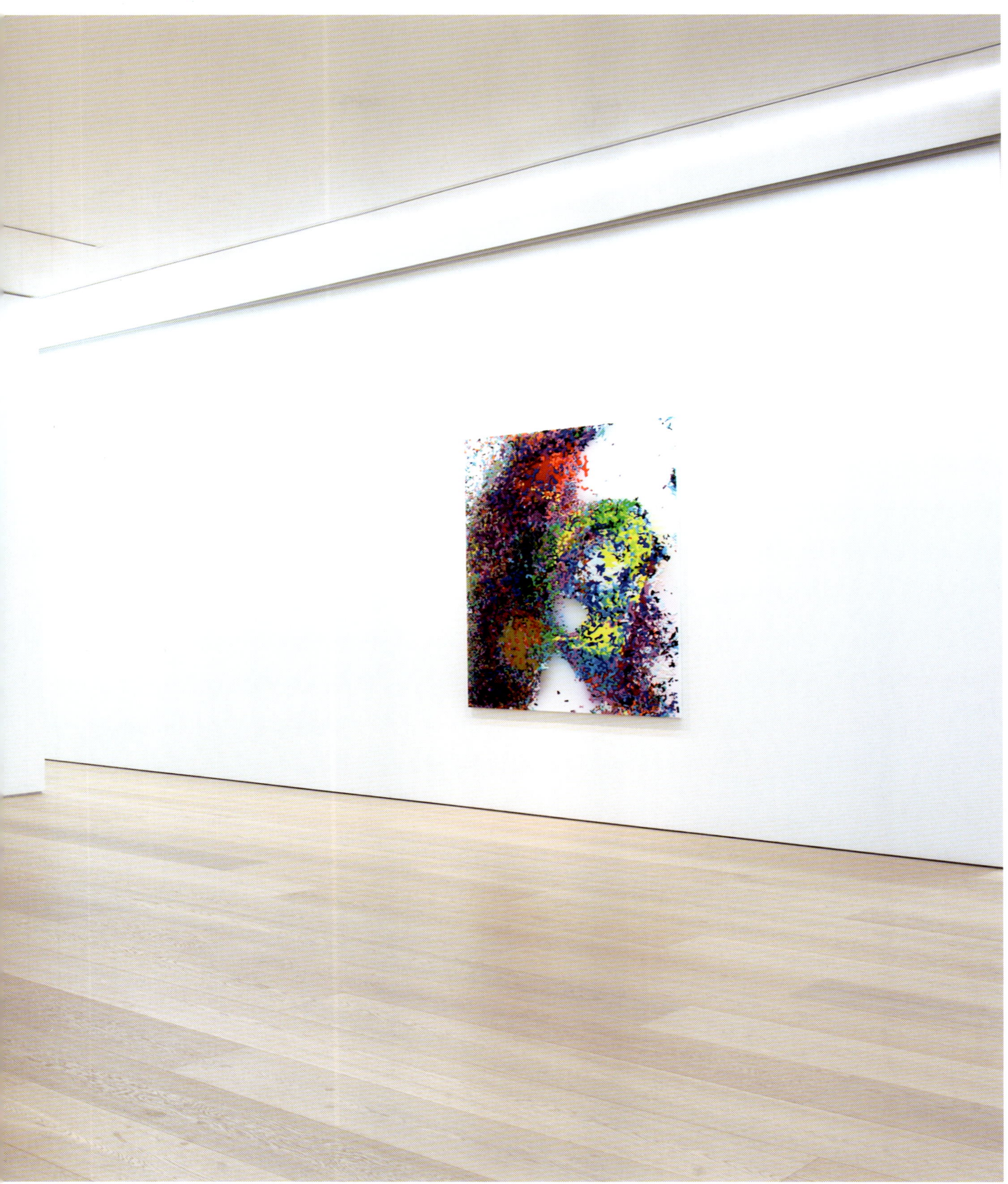

"滴 3 (drop 3)" 2012
Epoxy resin on canvas
150 x 110 cm / 59 x 43 1/4 inches

滴 3 2012 年
環氧樹脂帆布畫
150 x 110公分 / 59 x 43 1/4英吋

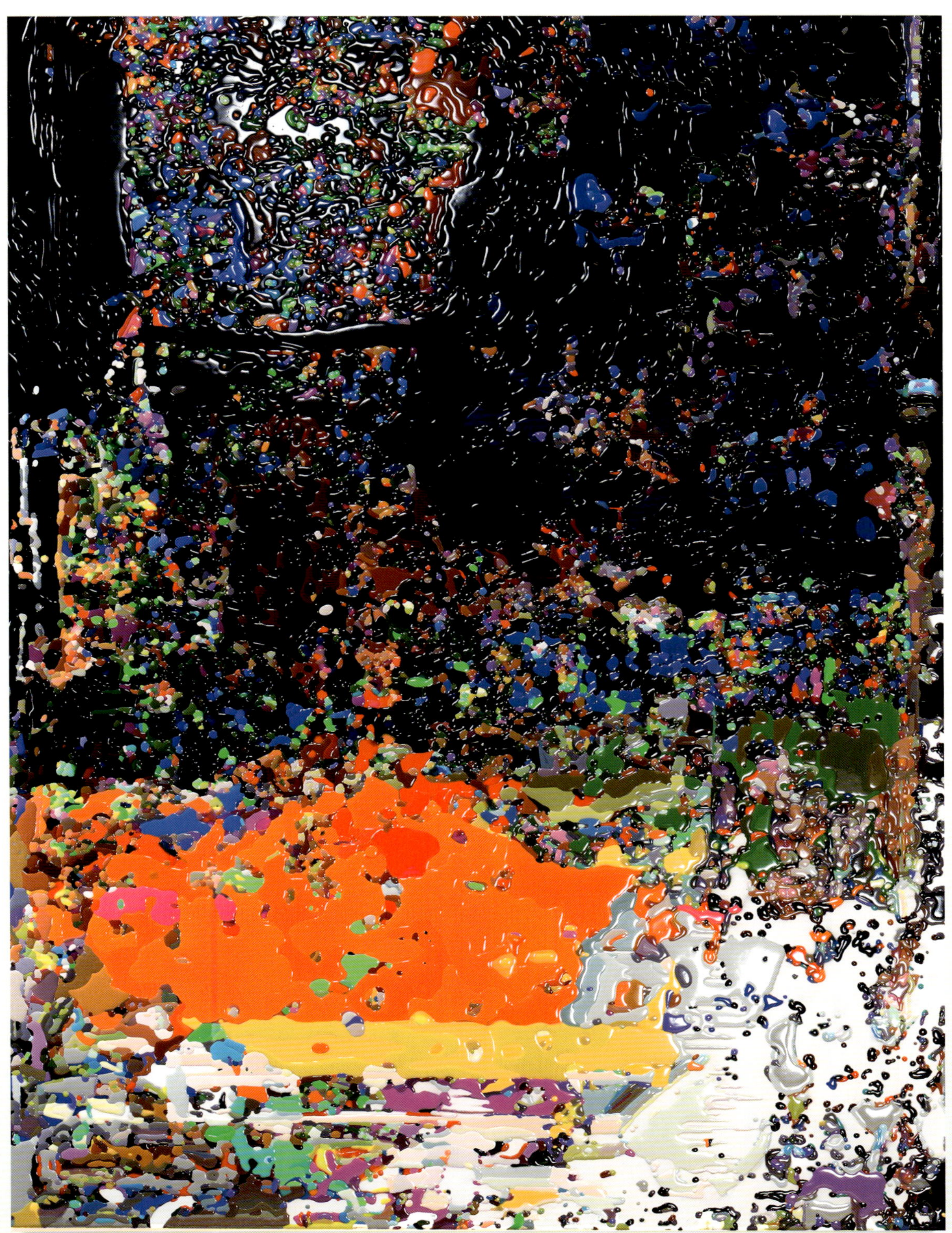

"滴 2 (drop 2)" 2012
Epoxy resin on canvas
150 x 110 cm / 59 x 43 1/4 inches

滴2 2012年
環氧樹脂帆布畫
150 x 110公分 / 59 x 43 1/4英吋

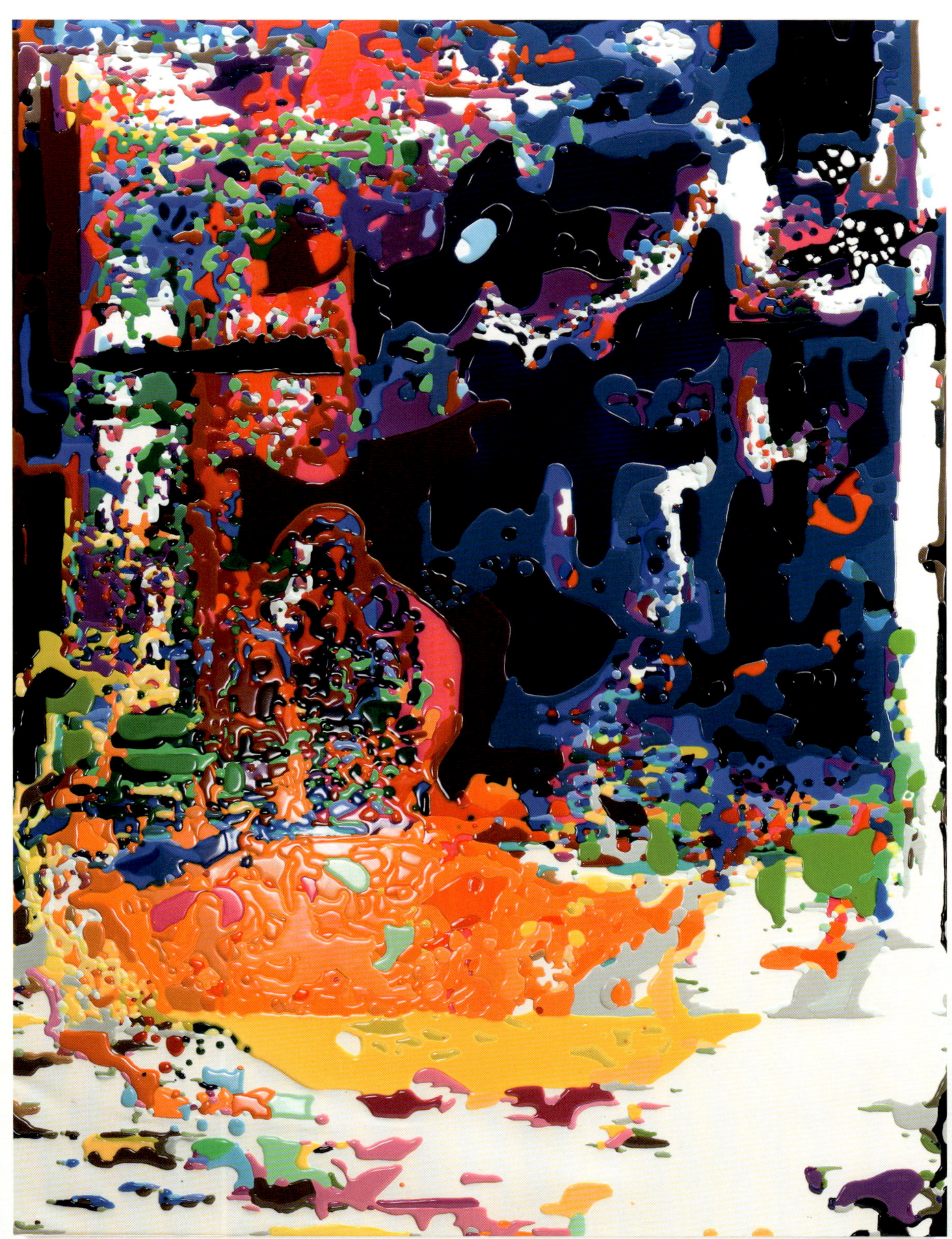

"滴 7 (drop 7)" 2012
Epoxy resin on canvas
150 x 110 cm / 59 x 43 1/4 inches

滴7 2012 年
環氧樹脂帆布畫
150 x 110公分 / 59 x 43 1/4英吋

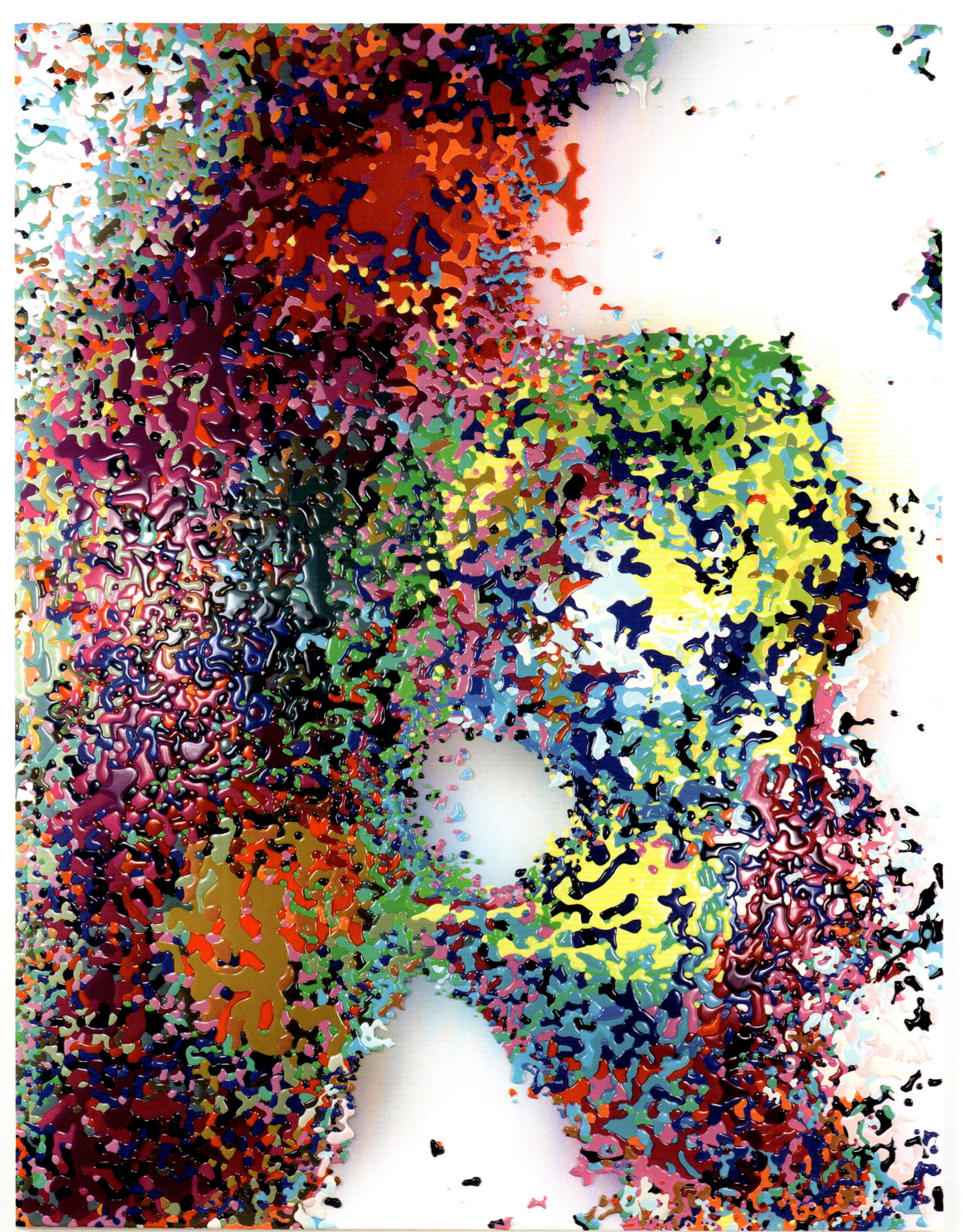

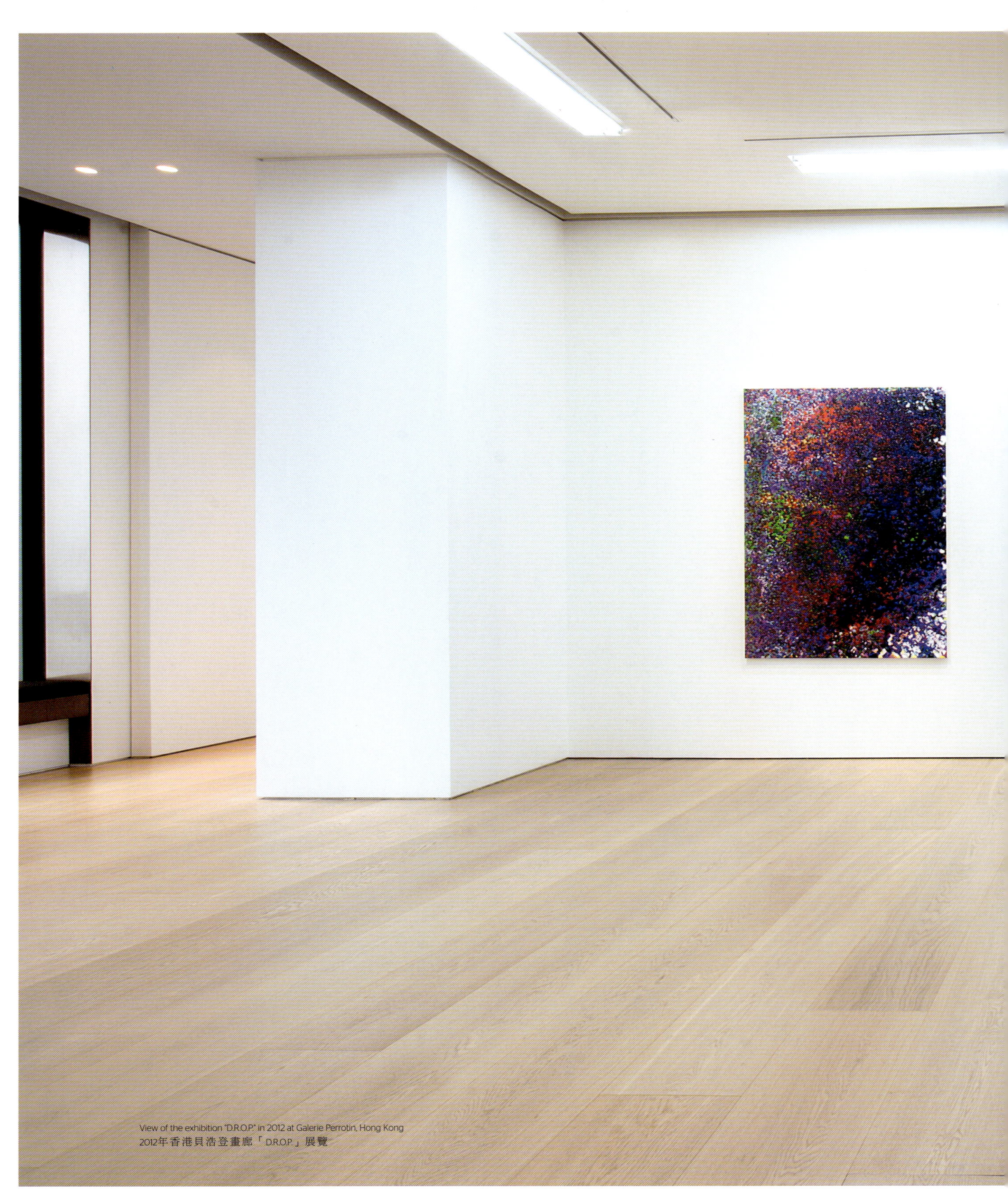

View of the exhibition "D.R.O.P." in 2012 at Galerie Perrotin, Hong Kong
2012年香港貝浩登畫廊「D.R.O.P」展覽

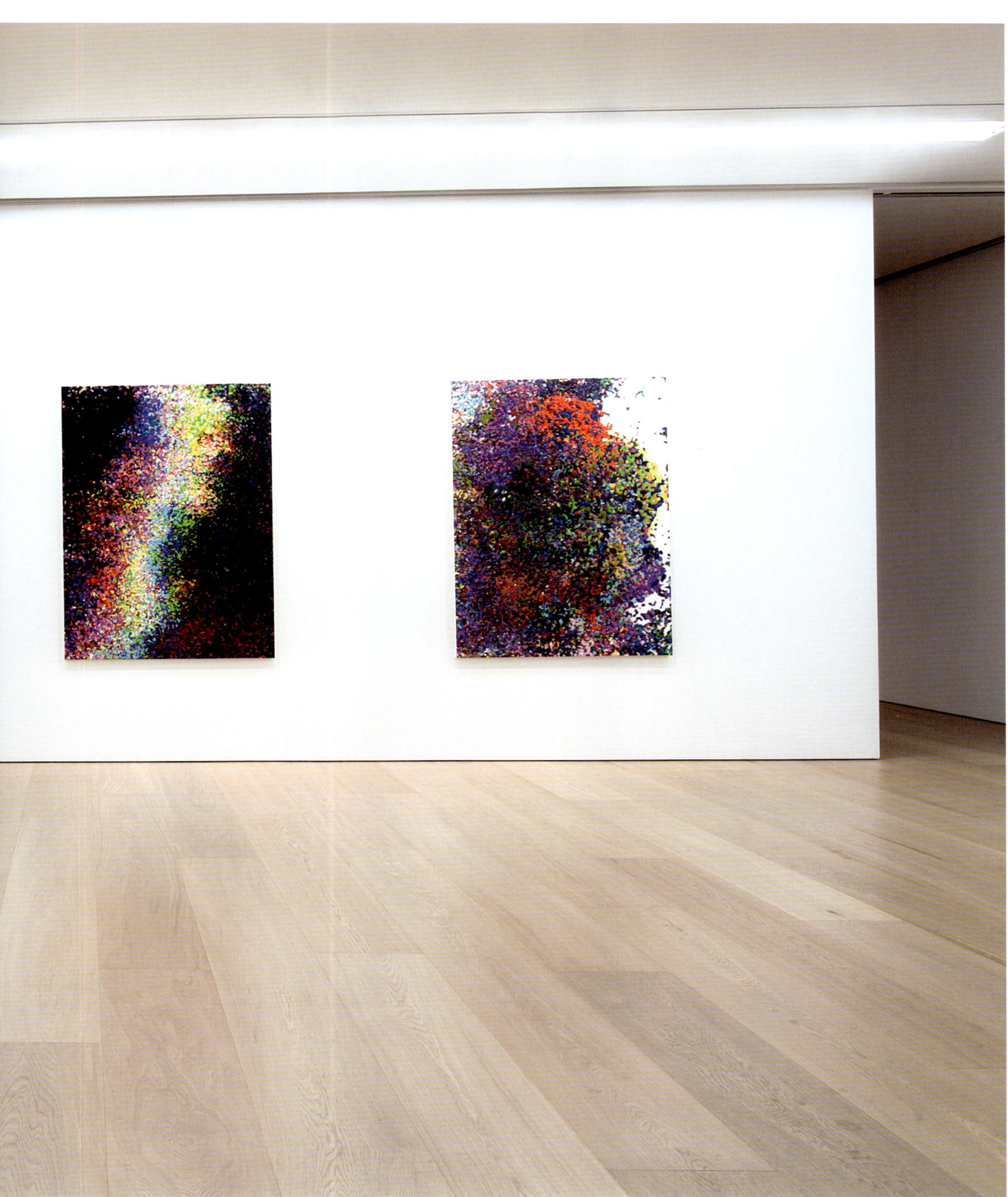

"滴 6 (drop 6)" 2012
Epoxy resin on canvas
150 x 110 cm / 59 x 43 1/4 inches

滴 6 2012年
環氧樹脂帆布畫
150 x 110公分 / 59 x 43 1/4 英吋

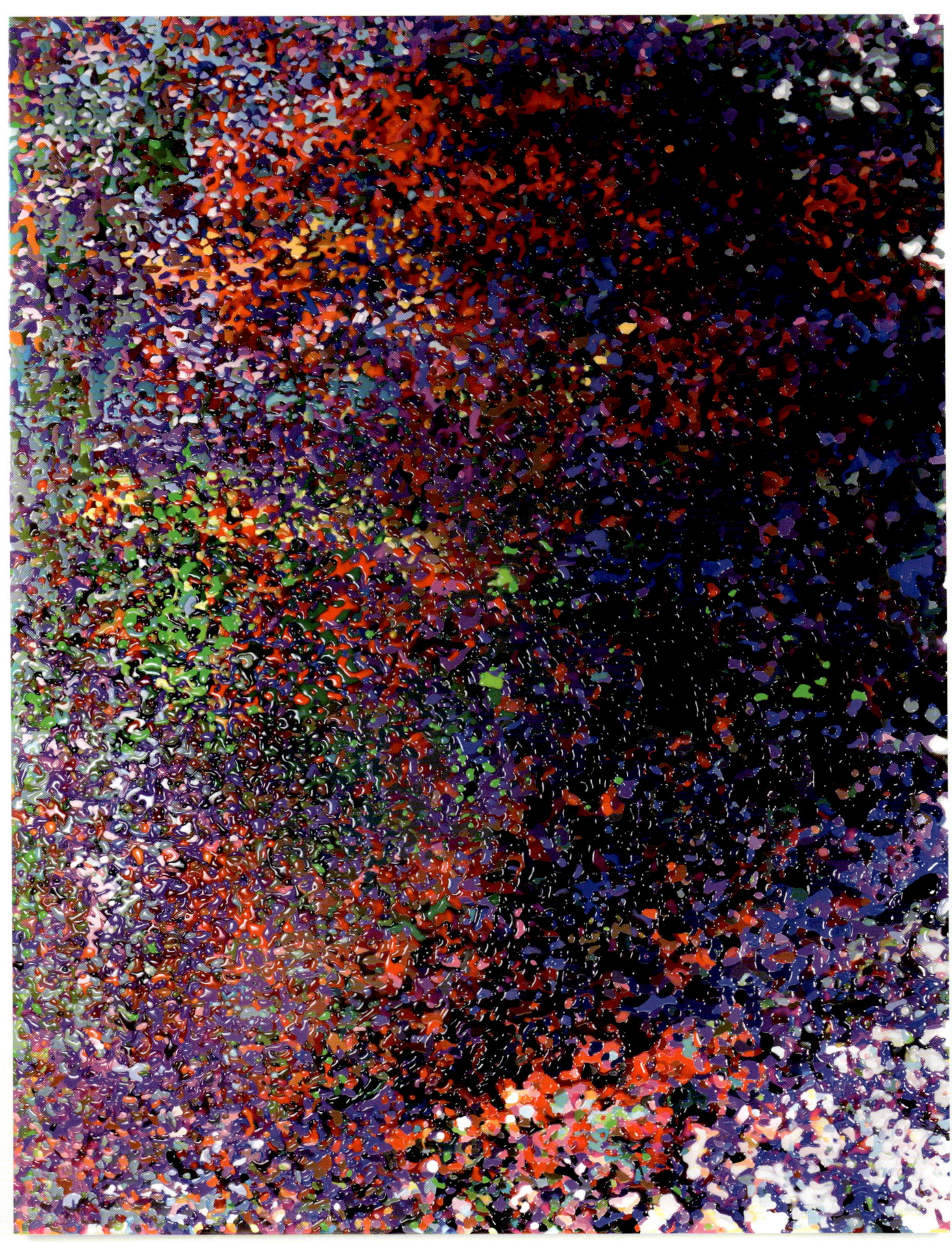

"滴 5 (drop 5)" 2012
Epoxy resin on canvas
150 x 110 cm / 59 x 43 1/4 inches

滴 5 2012 年
環氧樹脂帆布畫
150 x 110公分 / 59 x 43 1/4英吋

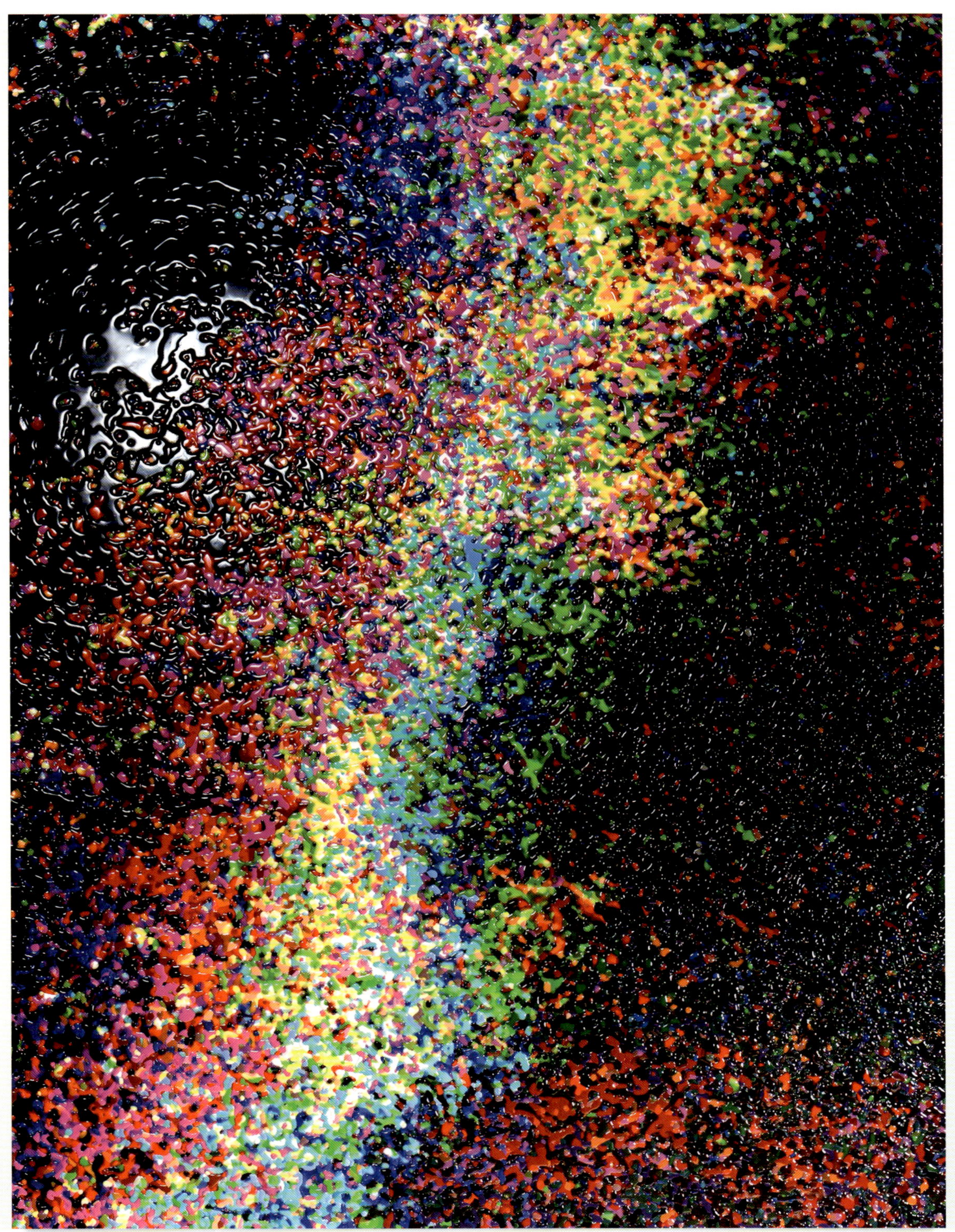

"滴 8 (drop 8)" 2012
Epoxy resin on canvas
150 x 110 cm / 59 x 43 1/4 inches

滴 8　2012年
環氧樹脂帆布畫
150 x 110公分 ／ 59 x 43 1/4 英吋

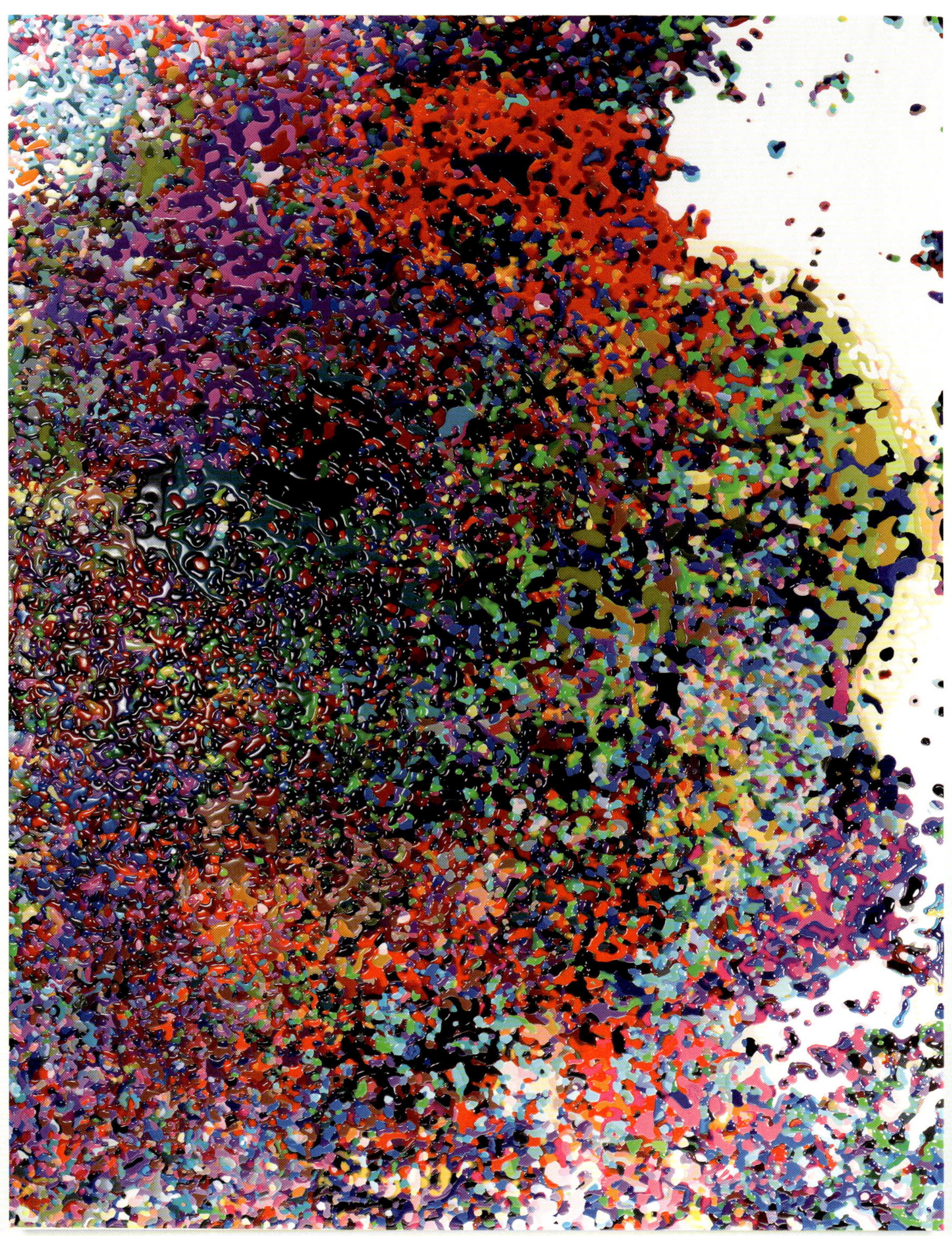

"滴 1 (drop 1)" 2012
Epoxy resin on canvas
150 x 110 cm / 59 x 43 1/4 inches

滴1 2012年
環氧樹脂帆布畫
150 x 110公分 / 59 x 43 1/4英吋

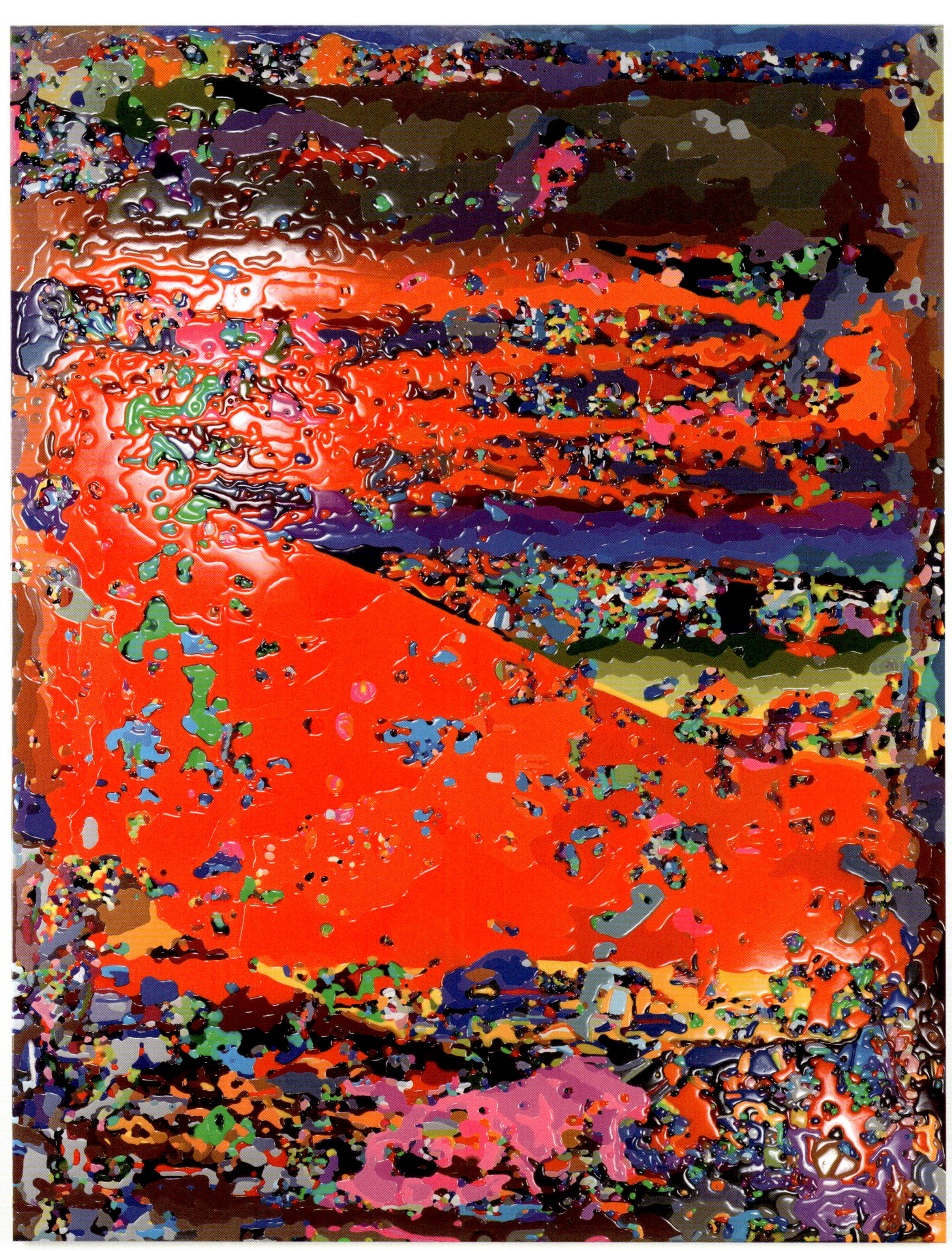

"滴 9 (drop 9)" 2012
Epoxy resin on canvas
150 x 110 cm / 59 x 43 1/4 inches

滴9 2012年
環氧樹脂帆布畫
150 x 110公分 / 59 x 43 1/4英吋

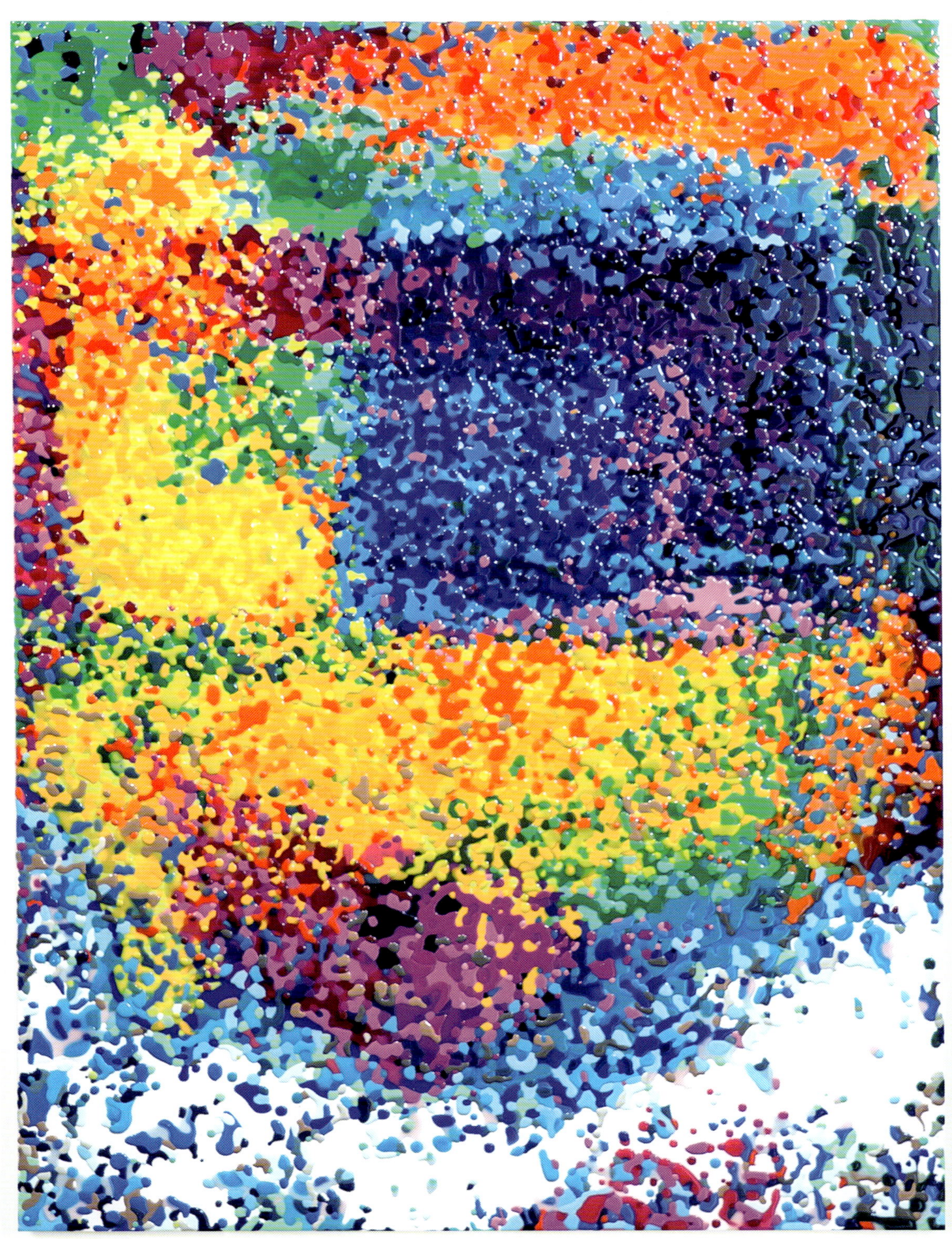

"滴 4 (drop 4)" 2012
Epoxy resin on canvas
150 x 110 cm / 59 x 43 1/4 inches

滴4 2012年
環氧樹脂帆布畫
150 x 110 公分 / 59 x 43 1/4 英吋

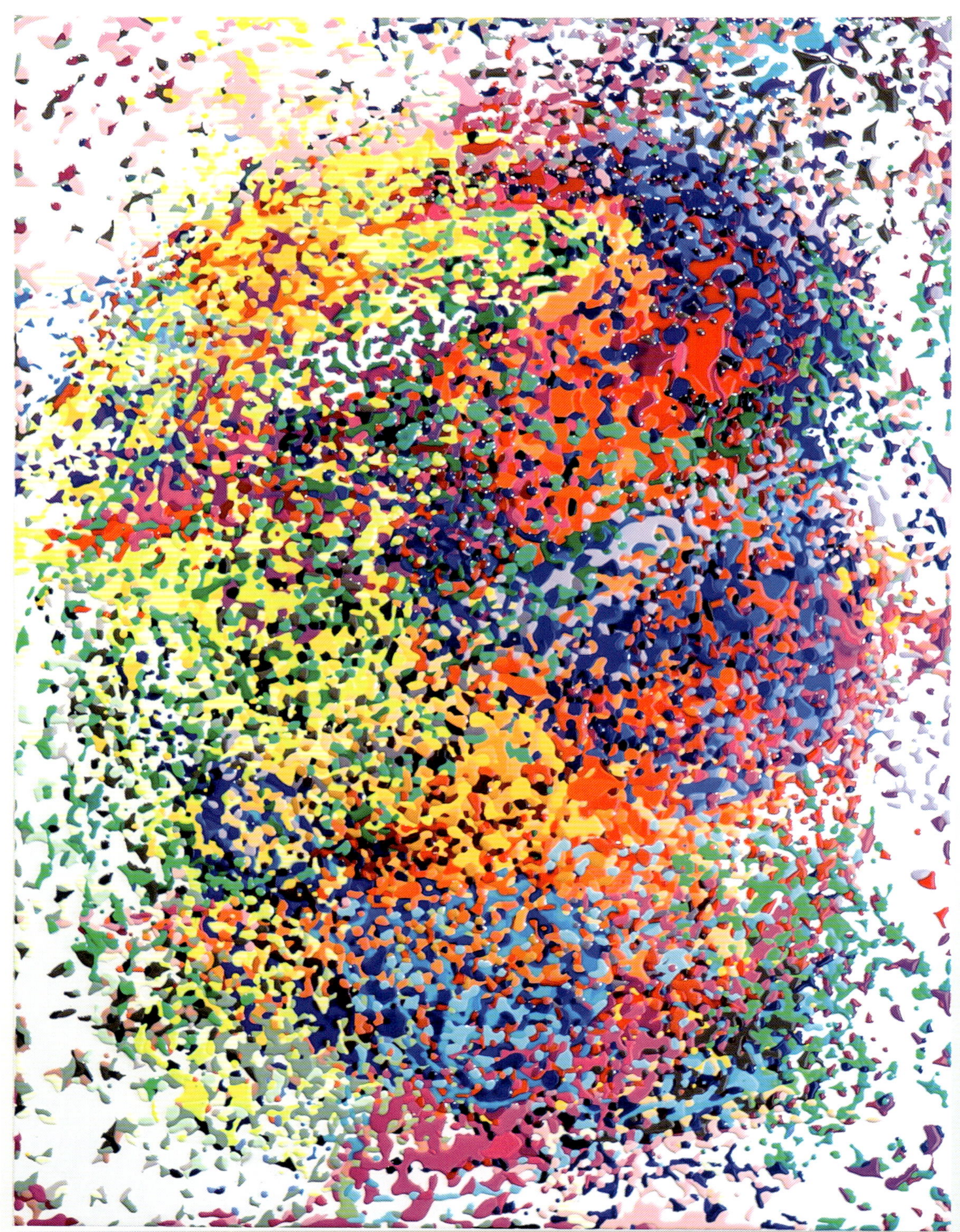

Coordination: Raphaël Gatel, Jeanne Briand, Clémentine Dupont, Philippe Joppin, Leslie You-Eyraud, Gerlinde Weber
Design: Sarah Suco Torres et Emmanuel Blondiau
Photography: Florian Kleinefenn, CAC Malaga, Ferdinand Neumüller, Allistair Overbruck, Thorsten Schneider, Laurent Segretier, Philippe Servent, Guillaume Ziccarelli, and others
Text: Marietta Franke
Translation: Aiwen Lu, Alan Yeung, Yuzhen Yao, Beauty Words

The artist wishes to thank Marietta Franke, Emmanuel Perrotin, Philippe Joppin and Laurent Segretier.

DAMIANI

via Zanardi, 376
40131 Bologna, Italy
t. +39 051 63 56 811
f. +39 051 63 47 188
info@damianieditore.com
www.damianieditore.com

GALERIE PERROTIN

www.perrotin.com

New York
909 Madison avenue
NY 10021 New York
newyork@perrotin.com

Paris
76, rue de Turenne
75003 Paris
Tel : +33 1 42 16 79 79
info@perrotin.com

Hong Kong
50 Connaught Road, 17th Floor
Central, Hong Kong
Tel : +852 3758 2180
hongkong@perrotin.com

Printed in May 2013 by Grafiche Damiani, Bologna, Italy.
ISBN 978-88-6208-307-2